The Busy Professor

Ten Easy Time Management Steps for Getting Your Academic Life Under Control

Timothy F. Slater, Ph.D.
University of Wyoming &
CAPER Center for Astronomy
& Physics Education Research

© 2018 Timothy F. Slater, *The Busy Professor*

Cover design by Amber Lynn Parker Richard

Editing by Megan Parker of Calliope & Quill

Author photograph by University of Wyoming Press Services

10 9 8 7 6 5 4 3 2 1

First Printing, March 2018
Second Printing, April 2018
Third Printing, June 2018

ISBN-13: 978-1986156288
ISBN-10: 1986156281

On the web at TheBusyProfessor.com
CAPER 604 So. 26th St.,
Laramie, WY 82070 USA
Email us at TheBusyProfessor@CAPERteam.com

Although the author and publisher have made every effort to ensure that the information in this book was correct at press time, the author and publisher do not assume and hereby disclaim any liability to any party for any loss, damage, or disruption caused by errors or omissions, whether such errors or omissions result from negligence, accident, or any other cause. The information in this book is meant to supplement, not replace, proper time management training. Like any activity, being an academic poses some inherent physical, emotional, and financial risk. The authors and publisher advise readers to take full responsibility for their safety and know their limits. Do not take risks beyond your level of experience, aptitude, training, and comfort level.

Because you really do want to spend more time with the ones you love

Table of Contents

1 ... PREFACE

5 ... TEN STEPS: Freedom comes from structure

17 ... STEP ONE: Rule your email

29 ... STEP TWO: Make TO DO lists that really matter

39 ... STEP THREE: Create a highly-structured syllabus

47 ... STEP FOUR: Don't break your writing appointments

55 ... STEP FIVE: Automate everything

65 ... STEP SIX: Put 20 seconds between you and your vice

71 ... STEP SEVEN: Pre-write letters, committee tasks, and grading comments

81 ... STEP EIGHT: Every talk or poster becomes a paper

87 ... STEP NINE: Use smart phone apps to build your CV

93 ... STEP TEN: Get a non-work life if you want to be more productive at work

97 ... NEXT STEPS: Beyond the TEN STEPS

BIBLIOGRAPHY

ABOUT THE AUTHOR

PREFACE

The ritual is nearly always the same.
>Salutation: "Hey, how are you?"
>Response: "Busy! How about you?"
>Conclusion: "Yeah, me too. Crazy busy!"

It seems that the response "busy" has become the new "fine" and is rarely questioned. Indeed, we are all feeling busy these days—*crazy busy*. Some of us are so busy that we wear our level of busyness and the length of our TO DO list as a badge of honor and status. It is as if the more things left undone on our TO DO list is a measure of our importance. Recently, I overhead a conversation where one busy professor was arguing with another busy professor about who was the busiest. Somehow, people have the idea that having a full calendar means that they are being successful at work, if not being successful at life. As it turns out, being busy does not equal success. The truth is, most of us work hard, but the levels of frantic activity we employ to get through the day are unhealthy. I believe too many of us feel too busy to be productive.

Are you too busy to read a book about time management? You might be, but you need to accept the harsh reality that being too busy is a choice. Don't you think I'm too busy to write a book about time management? Do you think the President of the United States is too busy to go to the gym? Derek Sivers, author of the book *Anything You Want*, eloquently argues that when a person says they are busy, that "'busy' implies that the person is out of control of their life." In response, this book is about one thing: helping you get your academic life under control so you can focus on doing the things that really matter to you.

To help with this task of getting your academic life under control so that you can be happy, productive, contributive, and have some satisfying sense of work-life balance, I want you to consider the following two professors, who both have a lot on their plates. The first professor we are going to call the "busy professor." This busy professor is characterized as being dedicated to their job and well-intentioned but a busybody with a full calendar of meetings, who only manages to find the time to complain about how busy they are in their flurry of frantic activity.

The second professor we are going to call the *Busy Professor*™ (and we will italicize it and put a trademark™ symbol on it to make this person seem super important). The *Busy Professor* is the scholar who dreams of a college professor's life as one where much time is spent reading journals, advancing intellectual arguments with colleagues and students, having free-time to write prolifically in archival journals, enjoying teaching highly motivated students, and providing national service as a leader in professional societies, all while minimizing day-to-day local committee grunt work, completing endless budget request forms, and begging mid-level administration for financial resources to do what ought to be done in outreach service to the region. Moreover, a *Busy Professor* has considerable time and freedom to do the hard work of scholarly thinking and is noticed and rewarded for their highly valued efforts and contributions.

You probably know where I'm going with this distinction and the honest question I'm about to pose to you. Which professor do you want to be? More to the point, which professor do you choose to be, because the decision really is yours to make every day. You must choose what is most important to you. Otherwise, you will just exist.

"A good man will not waste himself upon mean and discreditable work or be busy merely for the sake of being busy."
— Seneca

In the spirit of full disclosure, I've now read countless books on time management and research on what makes productive scholars so productive and shared what I've learned by mentoring thousands of faculty. In summarizing what I've learned, much of it through my own successful trials and flamboyant errors, I must be honest in saying I no longer know for sure which of these ideas are mine that I created from whole cloth, which I've adapted from the time management gurus, and which I have just plagiarized—the details seem to be lost in the mists of time. However, I suspect that there are few totally new ideas out there, so to be safe from the plagiarism-gods, I am going to claim that every idea here is unintentionally stolen from someone else, and I would appropriately cite them if I could only recall who said it first.

With that, let's take a walk, one step at a time, through the process of becoming the intellectually engaged *Busy Professor* you've always dreamed about being but just didn't quite know how.

Timothy F. Slater

TEN STEPS:
Freedom Comes from Structure

Overwhelmed. That's the only word I know that best describes how I felt. Not overwhelmed just once in a while, or once a week: I felt overwhelmed nearly every single second of every single day. I felt overwhelmed when I was frantically trying to meet some deadline only minutes away by madly pounding at my laptop keyboard or sending off one last hastily composed email full of misspellings from my smart phone while my airplane's boarding door was being sealed to leave the gate. My life was overshadowed by a foreboding sense that the dependably solid Earth beneath my feet would start crumbling away at any moment, and I would fall into the darkness. This feeling of being overwhelmed wasn't healthy and certainly didn't make me more productive or a better community member. The best-case scenario was I was about to burn out. The worst-case scenario was probably an early heart attack.

Mother Nature has numerous strategies in her natural disaster bag of tricks: avalanches, landslides, floods, hurricanes, tornadoes, wildfires, droughts, volcanoes, earthquakes, and killer asteroid impacts, just to name a few. But the disaster most like my life was that of a *tsunami*. Tsunamis—pronounced such that the beginning letter "t" is mostly silent—are often portrayed in popular movies as a towering tidal wave crashing against the shore, destroying everything in its path as a giant wall of water plows through. In actuality, tsunamis are much worse and many times more devastatingly deadly than that.

A tsunami is much more like a rapidly rising tide where the water, seemingly endless, keeps coming, and coming, and coming. Tsunamis are nearly impossible to survive. Unless you have an advanced knowledge that a tsunami is pending and a reliable action plan for survival, the relentless onslaught of water eventually overtakes you. You can't save yourself by climbing to a higher floor of a nearby building, because the water quickly erodes the lower floors, causing buildings to collapse. You can't hop in a fast car and outrun a tsunami, because the roads quickly fill with both debris and the unprepared victims succumbing to events, who turn into barriers and road blocks, preventing your escape. You can't cling to a palm tree or light post, because the never-ending flow of water eventually exhausts you. In fact, you can't even successfully use ropes to lash yourself to the trees, because the debris, caught up in the tsunami and drifting rapidly by, will pummel you to death. Tsunamis are deadly because the incursion of water is unceasing.

The day-to-day life of an academic often feels like being at the beginning of a never-ending tsunami. Academics must teach classes successfully; prepare and design effective instruction; answer student inquiries and provide timely assistance; grade assignments and give students meaningful feedback; integrate curriculum within and beyond their departments; submit end of term grades and forms, serve on hiring committees; conduct interviews; attend curriculum committee meetings; make strategic plans; provide service to the academic community by authentically serving on standing committees, ad hoc committees, peer-review committees, executive committees, and task forces; provide service to the extra-campus community in the form of outreach; work with schools; provide public lectures; respond to news media requests; respond to phone calls, text messages, and email-requests from others at the institution and beyond; build collaborations to create and submit grant funding proposals; nurture the scholarship of maturing students; attend frequent department meetings, college meetings, university meetings, and graduations; and…oh, yes, be a high-level, nationally known productive scholar, too. And don't forget, you also need to lead a balanced and reflective extracurricular life so that you can be healthy enough—physically and emotionally, that is—to participate in a family- and community-based life in meaningful ways.

Experienced academics are often so numb to the interminable list of daily TO DO items that they do not even realize how paralyzed and unproductive they have become. First, they stay at work later and later. Then, when that isn't enough, they arrive to their cluttered office earlier and earlier. Eventually, they start to miss their kids' soccer games, family reunions, and community festivals. And even when they are physically at home, they are mentally absent, still swimming in the tsunami's list of unfinished and upcoming TO DO items. The issue here with which successful, highly productive, and happy academics must contend is that paralyzing state of being "too busy to get anything done."

Believe it or not, there is a different academic life waiting for you—a rewarding academic life, where you can focus your intellect and cognitive attention on those areas that matter most to you. You can choose to be one of those rare academics who have figured out not simply how to survive the unabating academic tsunami, but how to flourish. These successful academics do not have easier jobs than you do, although they often make it look easy. They do not have picture-perfect personal lives that flow day to day without incident; they have unexpected challenges too. They are not lazy and irresponsible with their teaching because they would rather drink coffee at the shop in the Student Union with students or have a date to play tennis with a college donor. They are not on a lavish international vacation disingenuously disguised as a professional conference, noticeably absent while you are sitting in yet another useless committee meeting. Flourishing, productive, happy academics are indeed very busy, but not the same kind of 'busy' in which the majority of faculty immerse themselves. Instead, flourishing, productive, and happy academics have an action plan and a series of *gotta-do steps*—and *do-not-do steps*—that they are deeply committed to honoring.

There is a way for you to survive the academic tsunami. If you want a different life than the one you have right now—a happier and more productive one—then you must do something different than everyone else. If you want to have a better life than most of those around you, then you cannot do what they do every day in the way they do it. There are highly successful academics, and you can be one if you learn and implement the same survival strategies and action plans that the most productive academics use.

One Idea ...

To flourish as an academic, there is one single idea to comprehend, to accept, to explore, and to grok. It is a straightforward phrase that is easy to say and simultaneously difficult to embody. It is simply this:

FREEDOM COMES FROM STRUCTURE

Really? Such a phrase seems contradictory. How is it conceivable that living the academic life of freedom to do whatever a *Busy Professor* wants could possibly come from an externally imposed, restrictive structure? Allow me to explain.

One of the principle reasons that professors specifically choose an academic life is because of a sense of freedom, which is ubiquitous across academia. Academic freedom is the idea that academia is enhanced when scholars are free to explore and teach a variety of ideas and conduct creatively inquiries about the universe without being targeted for repression. In other words, academics can teach what concepts they think students need to understand, teach in a manner that they think will be most effective, and communicate the results of creative scholarship on the topics they find most interesting.

Now, to be clear, academic freedom is in no way carte blanche to do whatever one wants to do, or not do, all day long. Academic freedom carries with it the responsibility to serve the broader goals of the community. There are moral imperatives at play here: there are some common concepts professors agree to always teach; you must teach students in the most effective ways known; the domains of creative scholarship are subject to some larger value determinant. But with that caveat, professors often become professors because of some vague sense of academic freedom.

In a similar way, some people want freedom to arrange their schedules how they wish. Professors are not largely expected to be at their desk from 8 am to 5 pm, Monday through Friday, and off-campus evenings and weekends. In fact, it is quite the opposite. Many professors have teaching responsibilities in the evenings and community outreach responsibilities on weekends. The wide-ranging expectations exceeding the traditional 8-to-5 weekday workday for professors means that there is considerable flexibility in when you are expected to be on campus. Same goes for summer time. Generally, people think of this as highly desirable and an enormous benefit to being an academic.

More to the point, academics need quiet time to contemplate and create. Whether it is radically revising a course, developing a theoretical framework for a creative endeavor, or simply absorbing other scholarly ideas from the literature or conversation, these important tasks require time away from the daily whirlwind. Valuable ideas and insights do not always come during the 8-to-5 weekday workday when sitting behind a desk, so scholars need to have the freedom to think and create at inconvenient times.

What *Busy Professors* know that busy professors do not know is that given the freedom to do whatever you want, whenever you want, however you want, wherever you want, precious little will actually end up being accomplished unless specific structures are put in place. Although there is a fantasy narrative that academics live carefree, stress-free lives unbeholden to anyone, the actual day-to-day business of academia is so noisy that *Busy Professors* must build secure walls to keep out the inevitable distractions that come to us every day.

To be a flourishing *Busy Professor*, you need to build mental and physical structures that support doing what it is that you most want. If you fail, then what you most want to do will never be done. This is simply because the most important entries making up your curriculum vitae (CV) are products and activities that rarely ever have deadlines, things like highly-cited published papers and books, presentations at professional conferences, funded grant proposals, participation in national-level task forces, notable graduates, and teaching and mentoring awards. For certain, no one gets to list how many committee meetings they attended on their CV, or that they went to class everyday they were supposed to. In other words, the things you really want to do as a scholar and are uniquely privileged to do as a scholar are done on the timeline to which you set and adhere.

The first step toward being a *Busy Professor* starts with constructing a strict daily schedule that you really stick to. Now before you toss this book away in disgust, saying setting a rigid calendar isn't what you signed up for to be a *Busy Professor*, remember that you already have some strong skills at adhering to a schedule. You manage to make it to class when scheduled. You manage to make it to doctors' appointments when scheduled. You even manage to make it to the Dean's office on time when called to appear. And you can manage to pick up your friends from the airport or drop your kids off at school every day when scheduled. You do have the ability to stick to a schedule when it is important, and you don't really complain about it. This commitment to doing what academic-like things you most want to do also requires you to be on a schedule.

So, I'll say it again but this time with more enthusiasm: the first step toward being a *Busy Professor* starts with constructing a strict daily schedule that you really stick to. On this schedule you yourself create, you are going to schedule the things you really want to work on. This might be reading more journal articles, meeting with your most promising students, writing collaborative grant proposals for travel support and summer salary, or creating that book you've always said you wanted to write.

Let's consider an example. Many *Busy Professors* have teaching responsibilities, so setting aside time to do a great job teaching seems worthwhile to discuss as an example. The undeniable truth of the world is that you could spend 40 hours each week preparing to deliver *TEDTalk*-style lectures (everyone could always devote more time to their teaching). *Busy Professors* allocate a specific and reasonable amount of time to prepare their teaching, and when that time allocation is up, they do not stay later at the office to do more and miss dinner, or go back to working on their PowerPoint slides after their spouse goes to bed, or take their laptops to their kids' soccer games. Those things are what unhappy and unproductive busy professors do. *Busy Professors* do what they can do in the time allotted, and that has to be good enough. But to be clear, what *Busy Professors* do that busy professors do not do is actually work on their scheduled projects during their projects' scheduled time! They do not email during lecture-preparation time. They do not review memos or grant proposals during lecture-preparation time. They do not even grade or communicate with students during lecture-preparation time. *Busy Professors* work with purpose to finish the task they've assigned themselves, so that they can leave the office at a reasonable time, enjoy lengthy dinner conversation without distraction, and have a rewarding, non-academic life.

So, what does that really look like? First and foremost, *Busy Professors* always have an unchanging and productive morning ritual. You already have an unchanging morning ritual too, even though you might not realize it. Maybe it starts with the alarm going off, to which you groggily hit the snooze button. After snoozing, maybe you reach over and check your email on your phone. Go to the bathroom, brush your teeth, make some coffee, and check your smart phone again. Then off to work, sit down at your desk, look at your email yet again, dash off a few responses, take care of a few items on the giant TO DO list, and all of a sudden, to your great surprise, it is nearly noon. At this point, your day is gone, and your TO DO list is going to stay unfinished because nothing good ever seems to happen after lunch. And for busy professors, this happens every day, every day, every day.

Busy Professors know that they have complete freedom to do whatever they want to do, so they do what is most important instead of what is important to someone else. Daily rituals are as varied as the number of *Busy Professors* out there, but they often look something like this:

<u>4:45 am</u>: GET UP. Alarm goes off, no hitting the snooze, no looking at smart phone

<u>4:45 am-5:15 am</u>: Brush teeth, drink water, 10 minutes of simple meditation and blessing-counting, 10 minutes of simple yoga, and write down three things (just three) to get done today, while the coffee maker does its magic and your brain turns on

<u>5:15 am-6:30 am</u>: Work uninterrupted on a *Passion Project* (this book for example) and stop on schedule

<u>6:30 am-9 am</u>: Make your bed, have breakfast, maybe gym, get yourself and your family out the door peacefully, commute to work

<u>9 am-11 am</u>: Work only on projects that have no deadline, and build your CV; this time often involves collaborating with students

<u>11 am-1:30 pm</u>: Lunch & initial email time, perhaps scheduled meetings

<u>1:30 pm-3:00 pm</u>: Teaching responsibilities (lecturing, preparing, grading, innovating)

<u>3:00 pm-4:45 pm</u>: Scheduled meetings or phone calls, things that have deadlines, like budget reports or things your Chair or Dean have requested from you, and when time allows, some email

<u>4:45 pm</u>: STOP and LEAVE CAMPUS (*Busy Professors* always hard-schedule what time their day ends). Set an alarm and do not hit snooze

<u>Evenings</u>: Undistracted meal time with family and friends. Limited binge-watching of television. In bed by 9:30 pm, usually reading a real book on printed paper, avoiding the mesmerizing blue light from a smart phone, tablet, or television at all costs

 We will discuss the specific aspects of the morning ritual later, but there are three things I want you to notice. First, *Busy Professors* start their days early, even those who are devotedly "not a morning person." Not only are you at the peak of creative potential in the morning, but earlier hours grant your brain the most freedom from the unavoidable upcoming distractions of the day. Few of us can successfully be creative after being embroiled in the chaos of the work day. So, you are going to have to get up early and rule your mornings. *Busy Professors* do what busy professors don't do. Why lay in bed when there are dragons to slay?
 Second, the schedule includes things that are most important, like having a *Passion Project*. A *Passion Project* is something that you've always wanted to do, something that requires you to use focused energy to get it done well and moves you forward professionally. It is your primary "I'd really like to…" project that you need to make time for. It is one of those projects that will not get done if you do not make time for it to happen. The time is now. My current *Passion Project* is this book, and I work on it for no more than about 75 minutes every day. I

sometimes feel a bit like the plodding turtle in the *Tortoise and the Hare* story, but the number of words written really do add up quickly.

The third thing I want you to notice is that there are specific start and stop times in the schedule. *Busy Professors* know at what time they are leaving the office every day. *Busy Professors* know that they need to stop on time, even when things are going swimmingly well. If you stop working on a project when there is more left to write, then you will be able to get into it again the next day more quickly than if you had finished a section completely. In other words, leverage the adage, "Always leave them wanting more."

When you look back at your scholarly life, the things that really matter—intellectual engagements with colleagues and students, creating scholarly works of art, and building your CV for promotion and recognition—only happen if you purposefully create a time and space for these things to happen. Greatness and success do not happen by accident; they are won with strategy and discipline.

Here is a real example that *Busy Professors* encounter every day. Imagine you are in the middle of reading an insightful education research article on a new teaching method for your area. All of a sudden, seemingly out of nowhere, the interrupting thought boldly enters your mind: "Holy cow, I really need to grade those assignments from last week!" Whereas busy professors will put down the article for reading at some other time that will never actually occur, *Busy Professors* confidently say to themselves, "Yes, I do need to grade those papers and I have already allocated time in my schedule to grade at that time. Right now, this is my time I have scheduled to engage in the reading of this article. And because I made disciplined decisions to stay structured this morning, I will have free time later in the day to do whatever I want." Then with confidence and peace, the *Busy Professor* can go back to reading, knowing that grading will happen when it is intended to happen.

You have the freedom to choose if you are going to be an unhappy, reactive busy professor who tries to FIND time to get required things done or you can be the flourishing, pro-active *Busy Professor* that MAKES time to get important things done. In other words, if you want the freedom to go to your child's soccer game in the afternoon, you must commit to a strictly scheduled structure in the morning so that you can do what it is that is most important to you. Otherwise, you are starting your TO DO list at the end of the day instead of having it finished by noon. And you really can implement a structured strategy…but you need proven tactics that get you there. To keep you on track, we will explore the ten tactics, or steps, that you need to use to become a *Busy Professor*.

… and Ten Steps

Are you ready to be a highly productive and happy *Busy Professor*? I have a ten-step solution that will enable you to become both a flourishing academic *and* a meaningfully contributor to your community and family. To avoid the daily whirlwind of life that tries its mightiest to pull you off track, follow these ten steps:

STEP ONE: Rule your email

STEP TWO: Make TO DO lists that really matter

STEP THREE: Create a highly-structured syllabus

STEP FOUR: Don't break your writing appointments

STEP FIVE: Automate everything

STEP SIX: Put 20-seconds between you and your vice

STEP SEVEN: Pre-write letters, committee tasks, and grading comments

STEP EIGHT: Every talk or poster becomes a paper

STEP NINE: Use smart phone apps to build your CV

STEP TEN: Get a non-work life if you want to be more productive at work

As academics, it sometimes seems that our lives are uncontrollably subject to where the winds and the currents push us and our careers. This is simply untrue. Your pathway through this life is entirely up to you. The bulk of your academic life does not depend on luck; all of us have unlucky things happen to us. Your academic life does not depend on your salary; all of us wish we had more money. Your academic life does not depend on your Dean or Chair; few of us have an administrator that acquiesces to all our desires. Your academic life is in your hands.

Which type of busy do you want to be? Do you want to be the busy professor who runs from meeting to class to meeting, filling out budget forms and hastily created proposals before arriving home each evening too tired for family, hobbies, and meaningful reflection on life? Or, do you want to be the *Busy Professor* who is in full control of their academic life, making solid and intentional decisions about how to allocate their intellectual energy, making long-standing contributions to the academe that are highly valued, and being the enviable model of work-life balance? In the pages that follow, let me show you how to have the flourishing *Busy Professor* life you really do want to live.

Gotta-Do

Realize that you have tremendous freedom to choose how you allocate your intellectual and emotional energy each day

Get up early and work undisturbed on a deadline-free *Passion Project* a little bit every day that satisfyingly moves you forward professionally

Schedule what specific time you will start working on tasks and what specific time you will stop working on tasks

Create a morning ritual that you follow every day so that you control your highly valuable morning time before being swallowed by the inevitable after-lunch chaos

Avoid looking at your email before lunch at all costs, as the moment you do, you will get off-track

----

Step One:
Rule your email

If you can only get one time management strategy that works from all the books and workshops out there about time management and increased productivity, the single most important one to start with is about successfully managing your email so that your email doesn't manage you.

I am completely serious when I say that email is the most disastrous contribution of modern technology for academics (with, parenthetically, social media being a close second). In the *BM* era, before email, professors spent their time outside of class contemplatively reading books and articles at the library, intellectually arguing out ideas with colleagues and students, and thoughtfully writing down their ideas long hand. This is the sort of tranquil and erudite "professor-ing" that we dream about when we imagine what academia is supposed to be like. And by and large, academia was like this *BM*. Fast forward to today, and when we walk down the hall, we see professors hunkered down over their computers in their offices or thumbs madly pecking at a tiny smart phone screen, sending and responding, and sending and responding, and sending and responding to a relentless stream of emails, sometimes receiving hundreds per day.

When we were young and email was just starting to become more prevalent, we were told that email would save us time, email would save us money, email would make us more productive, and email would make collaboration easier. It was all a lie. In fact, email has done just the opposite. Email has taken us farther away from the professor-ing vision described above. Do you think your thesis advisor's advisor spent a better part of each day sending and responding to email and saying that there was not enough time in the day to create scholarship? They did not, and you do not have to either.

How much time do you spend every day checking your email? Studies show that on average people check their email 15 times per day. Moreover, I employed a motion-detection smart phone app that recorded me picking up my phone and turning on the screen more than 35 times per day. Our current addiction to notifications and emails is taking our time away from thinking, creating, and collaborating. Few of my colleagues even have hobbies anymore because they are so busy interacting with their screens.

How much time do you spend every day responding to email? How often has someone walked into your office for a meeting and you said something akin to, "Give me just a second while I finish up this email?" How much time do you spend every day sending email when you could just as easily pick up the telephone or walk down the hall and actually speak to someone? Here is my money-back guarantee: if you want more time for scholarship, then you've got to get your email use under control.

I know, dear reader, that you want me to hurry up and get to the "how to manage your email" discussion, but I suspect you've heard some of this before and it didn't stick. As a result, we should spend just a couple of minutes talking about why you are having trouble with your email. For reasons I do not fully understand, most of us suffer from some degree of urgency addiction. Instead of sitting motionless thinking deeply about an idea, it is easier to get a quick dopamine-rush from the action of receiving an email for which you get to respond. When you send email, you achieve the feeling like you are accomplishing something that you do not get when sitting quietly and thinking. Some of us even check our email accounts, unconsciously hoping that there might be a new message to respond to so that we can avoid doing the task we are supposed to be doing. The hard truth here is that you check your email because whatever is in there is hopefully easier than doing harder scholarly work. It is completely understandable that busy professors allocate time to email instead of the things that *Busy Professors* choose to spend their time and intellectual energy because it makes busy professors feel more like they are accomplishing something. Some harried busy professors even brag about how many emails they receive every day. On the flip side, flourishing *Busy Professors* brag about how *few* emails they engage with every day and how instead they spent their day adding to their CV.

With that preamble, we can now have a realistic "what really works" conversation about how to spend less time on your email.

Turn off email for just two hours a day

First, just STOP. I mean, really. Just stop. Turn off your email (and your smart phone) for two hours while you are doing something specific that doesn't have an immediate deadline looming. If you have never tried it before, beware—it is easier to say than to do. This shouldn't be that hard, but it is. You probably do not have your email notifications pinging you loudly while you are teaching for an hour (do you?). But somehow, when we are sitting grading a stack of papers, or reviewing a journal article, or otherwise doing something intellectual, most of us feel awkward if our email isn't turned on. This feeling resonates because most of us carry some nagging feeling that we are going to miss out on something really important, or that something will appear that would be more interesting and easier to accomplish in the next few seconds than the thing we are currently doing. In fact, as I sit here and write this passage, I quietly wonder what might be sitting in my email (*Are lottery winners notified by email?*). But I know if I dare open my email program, then I won't finish this paragraph.

Our students are convinced they can multitask—turns out, they can't. Unproductive busy professors think they can multitask—turns out they can't multitask either, even though they are pretty good at rationalizing it. Busy professors have their email on constantly, waiting for something important to show up. Instead, productive *Busy Professors* know that "task switching" is a huge impediment to meaningful productivity, so they purposefully put specific barriers in place to ensure that they are not disturbed by their email (or cell phone).

What does "turn it off" actually look like? To my mind, there are five progressive levels of *Busy Professor* email barriers. Novice *Busy Professors* start slowly at level one and move their way up to being more and more daring once they realize two incredibly valuable things: one, you don't miss anything critically important, and two, you are amazed by how much more productive you are. The reward is rewarding!

LEVEL 0: Email is on constantly and you notice every "receive"
LEVEL 1: Turn off your email for at least one hour per day
LEVEL 2: Don't access your email before noon
LEVEL 3: Don't access your email before 3pm
LEVEL 4: Set your email to SEND/RECEIVE only once a day

  The most frequent objection I hear when I talk about these progressive levels of email detachment from busy professors is, "What if my Chair or Dean calls an emergency faculty meeting?" Well, I can't prevent chaos from happening; however, I can promise you that if an emergency meeting is called, I am certain my colleagues will stop by my office on their way down the hall to ask me to speculate what I think the recently-announced-mystery-urgent-meeting might be about, thus telling me that there is an unscheduled meeting about to occur. My repeated evidence for this is that many of my colleagues stick their head in my door or catch me in the hall and give the busybody busy professor's universal salutation greeting: "Say, did you get my email?" This in and of itself provides sufficient assurance to me that I won't miss anything.
  The second most frequent objection to turning off email by busy professors is, "What about urgent student requests? My students are always plugged in and expect me to be responsive!" This is potentially a real issue for busy professors and *Busy Professors* alike because our end-of-course student evaluations often have a question that asks about instructor availability and responsiveness. However, I have found that busy professors with a wide-open door policy and who will never skip out on five minutes of office hours to go to the bathroom have the same results on this availability item as their overall rating score. In other words, your availability score is largely independent of how available you truly are, within reason. More to the point, if your students perceive by your behavior that you are overall too busy, they probably conclude that you do not actually have time for them or are personally uninterested in their success, regardless of how available you are.

The *Busy Professor*'s solution to being responsive to students while also not having their email on constantly is a straightforward, three-step process. The first step for *Busy Professor* is to separate out class-related email from students from your regular day-to-day email. I did this by going to a free online email service (I happened to use Google's Gmail) and set up a teaching-only email I aptly named *SlaterClass@gmail.com*. This step is important because you want to be able to work on your class-related emails all at one time and in one place, and not students' emails interrelated and intermixed with departmental policy emails, research-oriented emails, personal emails, and spam-related commercial email. I repeatedly tell my students to please use this special *SlaterClass* email when they email me, or it is likely that their email will get lost in all the junk and spam I receive from my university, and I do not want their email to get lost. I offer this as one of the ways I am trying to help them succeed and remind them that their email is important to me. I also suggest they put their course and section number somewhere in the subject line so that I can easily find their email. And in the surprisingly rare event I do receive a student email at my regular .edu email account, I simply forward it to my teaching email account and deal with it at a purposefully scheduled time when I am thinking about class-related issues and not distracted by something else. Whereas the harried busy professor appears overwhelmed and thus unavailable to students, a well-structured *Busy Professor* radiates availability and the sense of being highly interested in setting up clear pathways for their students' success.

The second *Busy Professor*'s step is to repeatedly tell your students that you only check your email every other day. My repeated experience with thousands of students—I often teach incredibly large lecture classes with hundreds of students in each section—is that students are generally okay with you being a bit slower returning their emails if they can be assured that you will get back to them. I learned to my surprise that many college and university student-exit polls show that the second most common student complaint is that their professors never return emails or phone calls. (The most common complaint, if you are curious, is usually about limited parking.) In other words, I clearly tell my students that I will respond every other day and to expect a response within 48 hours. By managing students' expectations, I assure my students that their success in the class is important to me. To further support this assurance, I also set up an auto-responding vacation message on my teaching email that says I will respond. Please feel free to use my auto-responder in your own email.

Auto-Response from SlaterClass@gmail.com
Hi! Thanks for your email. I only check my email about every 48 hours during the week, so please know that I will get back to you. If you haven't heard from me within 48 hours, feel free to email me again (unfortunately, things do get lost now and again). If you have a question, you might also get your question answered more quickly if you ask a classmate, as they might know the answer.

If this is an emergency and really can't wait, please feel free to telephone me on my personal cell phone (please do not text me), as long as it is at a 'reasonable hour.' A reasonable hour is defined as a time of day when my wife won't get mad at me or you for my telephone ringing and waking her up. If she gets mad at me, I won't be as friendly to you as I otherwise would be!

Thanks again for writing to me,
TSlater

email: slaterclass@gmail.com

reasonable hours personal cell phone number:
520-975-1374 (please don't text me)

Note that I give students my personal cell phone number. Before you object, you should know that I have given my personal cell phone number to thousands of students, and I have never had a student abuse this. It is possible that I have just been lucky. On the other hand, I give students my personal cell phone number with several caveats. First, I make it clear that this is my personal number, and that it is only to be used in dire emergencies. Despite countless hallway jokes to the contrary, students do seem to know what this means. Moreover, when I say personal number, I am emphasizing that I am there if they need me.

Second, I clearly specify "do not text me." I imply that I don't text; however, the truth is that contemporary students will readily email a professor or text a professor in the middle of the night but are for some reason highly reluctant to make an actual voice telephone call. Even when not an emergency, when was the last time you received a voicemail from an undergraduate student? See my point?

Third, I invoke the "angry spouse" warning about my personal cell phone. I tell my students during class, on my syllabus, and in my auto-responding email that they may call me "*...as long as it is at a 'reasonable hour.' A reasonable hour is defined as a time of day when my wife won't get mad at me or you for my telephone ringing and waking her up. If she gets mad at me, I won't be as friendly to you as I otherwise would be!*" This approach has always worked for me (knock on wood), and I offer it to you as my hard-won experience.

Stop Sending Email...*if you want to receive less*

Ever wonder why you get so much email? I mean, several decades ago, a professor might get a couple of letters a day, but never ever hundreds of correspondences each day. The immediate response most people conjure occurs because emails are so quick and easy to send, as compared to hand-written postal correspondence—which is absolutely true, and a fact that thriving *Busy Professors* leverage to keep their email inbox flow relatively small.

You might be surprised to learn that the amount of email you get is directly related to the amount of email you send, commercial-advertisement email aside, although you can somewhat limit that too. If you can, I want you to think back to when you were at a professional conference or multi-day retreat or vacation where you had limited access to the Internet. If you count how many emails you received that week and compare it to this week, I guarantee you that you received more email this week. How do I know this? Because a beautiful correlation exists between the number of emails you send and the number of emails you receive. What I am suggesting here—with actual data—is profound. The reason you get a crazy amount of emails is your own fault: the reason you get too many emails is because you send too many emails, and it is only made worse by you furtively sending emails from your smart phone during meetings.

After recovering from the shock of this revelation—and after you go into your own email inbox and sent mail folders and try, unsuccessfully, to disprove me—consider this easy-to-implement *Busy Professor*'s solution:

*Busy Professor*s strive to leverage "LEVEL 4: Set your email to SEND/RECEIVE only once a day." You will be surprised how productive you can be when you set your SEND/RECEIVE function to once per day. When your email is in this setting, you can load up as many sent emails as you like, but they are only distributed at the time you specify. I recommend setting it to 3 pm. This way, a bunch of emails do not arrive onto your desk until 3 pm when you are mentally past your daily creativity burst, and it is a good time to deal with email. Further, you can easily see which of your colleagues are most addicted to their email, because you'll have a flurry of responses from busy professors by 3:20 pm. And most importantly, since you won't actually be distributing your email responses to these newly acquired emails until the next day, you will dramatically decrease the amount of email passing through your day.

Will you miss something? Yes. You will miss the unnecessary and constant back-and-forth that busy professors spend all day engaging in. When people get used to you only responding to email in the afternoons, they learn that if it is something time-critical, they can pick up the telephone and call you. In fact, *Busy Professors* make it a practice to constantly tell colleagues that they are terrible at keeping up with email—and texting—and forget to check email. Effecting a reputation of being absentminded when it comes to email is a useful strategy here. *Busy Professors* remind colleagues that if something is critically time-sensitive to please make a telephone call on their personal cell phone. By nature, people these days are reluctant to call a personal number and interrupt you, so they usually make the decision to wait unless they cannot. The result is an invaluable enhancement to a *Busy Professor*'s productivity, and you are guaranteed not to miss anything critical.

Send Email Only If You Must...*and do so politely*

Too many of my busy professor colleagues are frantically trying to bang out as many emails per minute as possible. You can imagine their exhausted fingers flying madly across the keyboard, maybe fixing misspellings (maybe not), and certainly not taking the time for even the most basic rules of politeness. I am too often politely reminded by my Latin American colleagues that it is rude to start any conversation before authentically querying, "How are you?"

Busy Professors use the rule, "If one does not have the time to write a polite email, one does not have the time to check their email." You either have time to include a salutation and something, or you do not have time to email. It might momentarily feel good to ring up a bunch of rapid kills in your email response, but it is completely unfair to the person who took time to email you to simply "dash off" a quick, sentence-fragment response.

Dear Pat: Thanks for your email, how wonderful to hear from you. Hope things are going well (Me? I'm just busy trying to stay out of the wind, as it always messes up my hair). By the way, you did a nice job on that presentation last week. I appreciated the time you took to find that data. As to your question, …

<insert response>

I know you're busy. So, NRN (No Reply Necessary). If you need an additional explanation, feel free to give me a call on my personal cell phone, as I am rarely good at keeping up with my email.

Commit to OHIO

I know this chapter has gone on quite a while—but I believe getting your email under control is the first and most impactful strategy that *Busy Professors* use to live the productive, intellectual life they most desire. So, my last tactic here, committing to OHIO, explores what to do when you are working on your email. I don't mean commit to living in the Buckeye state, Ohio, but instead commit to living the principle embodied in the acronym O.H.I.O.: *Only Handle It Once*.

OHIO is a time-tested secret strategy among people that handle and pass through high volumes of digital and hard-copy paperwork. But for productive *Busy Professors*, it particularly applies to processing their email inbox.

Only Handle It Once means that *Busy Professors* never open an email unless they have time to deal with whatever it says. Now, to be honest, there are some email requests that require considerable intellectual energy and time to fully respond to. I propose, however, that such emails don't show up as frequently as you might think. I know you have one in mind, perhaps treading water in your email inbox right now. But these traumatic email events are louder in our selective memories than they deserve to be and interfere with our ability to make productive, overarching, strategic decisions on how to best be a *Busy Professor*.

Whenever I open an email, I do one of four things to it. Most commonly, I delete it. Sometimes, I can't bear the emotional stress of deleting an email that might become important someday, so I perform my second email action and drag it into a folder I created called Archive. I have never actually had to go back into my Archive folder for something, but I am convicted to the idea that I might someday. The third action I take is to respond, but only if I can within about two minutes. The fourth action is to drag the email into a folder I created called Action-Required. This action is invoked when the email request is going to require some thought or background research, and I can't deal with it within two minutes.

Busy Professor OHIO Email Actions
1. Delete it
2. Archive it
3. Respond to it, if can be done within 2 minutes
4. Move it into an *action-required* folder

Limiting myself to only four possible actions is incredibly liberating—and fast. *Busy Professor*s can process an entire inbox of 150 new emails in about 20 minutes using this strategy. Then, with the remaining time I have allocated to responding to email, I can deal thoughtfully with the emails sitting in my Action-Required folder. The process allows *Busy Professors* to be thoughtful and appropriately responsive to the emails that really do deserve their attention without worrying about what might be lurking in the next unread email.

By implementing these tactics, you can get your email under control and do a better job of keeping the main thing the main thing in your life. As a first-step place to start being a *Busy Professor*, consider committing to the following *Gotta-Do* list. As end of chapter homework, you might consider what your list of *Do-Not-Do* commitments related to your email might be.

Gotta-Do

Turn off your email notification sounds so that your computer and smart phone do not distract you when another email arrives

Stop sending so much email—pick up the phone or walk down the hall. Or, send at least one hand-written note each week

No casual email-checking. Be purposeful with your email and commit to OHIO: Only Handle It Once

---

STEP TWO:
Make TO DO lists that really matter

People have been using the strategy of creating a written TO DO list to remind them of what all needs to get done since the invention of paper and pencil, and probably longer. Like grocery shopping lists, you probably have several TO DO lists right now scattered among your desk detritus. To be certain, there isn't anything wrong with creating a TO DO list—most *Busy Professors* use them all the time. The problem is that busy professors do not use these lists effectively.

To get right to the point, there are things busy professors do that *Busy Professors* strive to avoid, and you should too. One is that busy professors have TO DO lists that are far too long to ever be accomplished. When not paying attention to the productive ways of the *Busy Professor* myself, I have created two column lists that go on for pages. Such an approach might be good for the initial planning stages for running a large professional conference or for brain-dumping a lot of ideas, but this sort of interminable list never works on a day-to-day basis. To further add weight to the notion that TO DO lists don't work well, consider that software companies providing online TO DO lists are able to track the "done-ness" of these lists across thousands of users, and they generally report that only about 40% of entered tasks are ever marked as completed.

There is a second reason to avoid creating long TO DO lists: hopelessly busy professors can unintentionally become obsessed with crossing as many items off their TO DO lists as possible. What can happen is that busy professors use the number of crossed off list items as a measure of their value, and their goals become crossing off items to make themselves feel better, instead of crossing off items to move toward their goals. This occurs when busy professors confuse the feeling of frantic activity with that of authentic productivity. Such a notion is like the busy professor who cannot get around to submitting a journal manuscript because their calendar is too full of meetings. Busy professors are often so busy that they cannot get anything accomplished, and long TO DO lists support this pathway.

> "Those who are wise won't be busy, and those who are too busy can't be wise."
> — Lin Yutang, *The Importance of Living*

The best TO DO lists are short and reflect purpose
*Busy Professor*s do something different with their TO DO lists than their overly busy colleagues. *Busy Professors* certainly have TO DO lists, but the items are always written with specificity. Instead of some vague reminder item that says, "Call Pat," *Busy Professors'* items say something more like, "Invite Pat to serve on panel discussion at fall conference." Just like the dreadful worry of an unopened email with who-knows-what lurking in its words, a vague TO DO item does not actually remind one of what is to be done. The best TO DO items reflect both an action step and the purpose.

As an overly simplistic example, imagine that you have been asked by a colleague to teach their class for a day while they are off to a meeting. Rushing out the door to catch a flight, a busy professor would breathlessly ask you to "teach 'clouds' tomorrow." This really isn't very helpful. What you need to know is what students did last week and what students will do the following week, so you can sequence the class appropriately. The same goes for an effective TO DO list.

Before you write this off as being silly, this seemingly insignificant idea becomes critically important when *Busy Professors* decide how to prioritize the items on their TO DO list. *Gotta-do* items are those that move *Busy Professors* toward their main goals, especially those items that do not have urgent deadlines and add important lines to a *Busy Professor's* ever-growing CV. You need to be able to critically review your list to determine if you are focusing your energy on the things that are the most important things, or if you need to change your approach. This is even more important if you are working with a mentor, as this gives them a place to provide solid, actionable advice. TO DO lists really do need to reflect purpose.

Consider for just a moment how you set your priorities for deciding how to allocate your limited time. You do not have time to do everything you could do. But you do have time to do what is a priority for you. Try this thought experiment the next time you are trying to decide if you have time to do something or haven't been able to make time for something seemingly important. Instead of saying to yourself, "I haven't had time to get around to doing that yet," try saying to yourself instead, "It's not a priority," and see how that feels. Sometimes it will feel perfectly fine. For example, "I have time to alphabetize my files, I just don't want to." But other things are many times more complicated. Imagine saying, "I'm not going to edit a graduating student's CV because it's not a priority" or "I don't go to the DMV because my having a driver's license is not a priority." You really do have a choice about how to spend your time and intellectual energy. If you don't like how you're spending your day, *Busy Professors* have the unique job-structure that lets you choose a different daily pathway.

Characteristics of *Busy Professors'* TO DO Lists
- ✓ Short, usually three items TO DO to be done today
- ✓ Prioritized, noting which one will be done before lunch
- ✓ Clearly reflect what is valued
- ✓ Use a simmering pot or tickle-file list to capture long-term todays
- ✓ Simple and require little if any maintenance
- ✓ Do not require luck or good fortune to be completed

Do not create TO DO items that require luck or good fortune

Over the history of your own TO DO lists, you probably notice that some get done and some do not get done, but have you ever noticed why this occurs? Flourishing *Busy Professors* only put down TO DO items that are going to get done.

My experience is that *Busy Professors* can only reliably get three important TO DO items done each day, and sometimes it takes real discipline to get even one of those three things done. I'm not talking about list items, like "go to class" or "go to committee meeting"—these things go on your daily calendar. Instead, I'm talking about career-influencing important things that eventually end up on a CV that rarely have urgent deadlines, like "outline discussion section to analysis paper," or "give feedback to co-author Chris' conference presentation proposal."

    A *Busy Professor*'s three-item daily TO DO list also has a single item starred as being most important to get done that day. Let's face it, once you get to the office and start to interact with colleagues and students, things start to get frantic. And if you dare to open your email, you will always, always get sucked into some manifestation of, "Your poor planning isn't my emergency." Some people call this the "work whirlwind" and it is very difficult not to get caught up in it. Your goal is to stay out of the work whirlwind as long as you can. You can probably hold it off until lunch if you stay away from your email, but even the best of us can't hold it off all day, every day. Therefore, *Busy Professors* make sure that they structure their day so that at least one of their three carefully selected TO DO items is done before lunch. Time-tested strategies to do this include: not stopping by the departmental office upon arrival, keeping your office door closed until your single most important TO DO item is completed, avoid scheduling morning meetings, and not opening your email until after lunch. When given the rare luxury of choice, *Busy Professors* prefer to teach (and prepare to teach) in the afternoon time slots, leaving their mornings free to work on creative scholarship when their minds are not clouded with the daily whirlwind caused by their overly busy colleagues.

Email is the TO DO list killer

    You thought we were done talking about email, given that it was the longest chapter in the book, but email engagement will destroy even the most diligent *Busy Professor's* day. This is because 90% of the email professors receive does not help them move forward; instead, most of it is a TO DO request for someone else. If you've ever noticed during an FAA-required safety briefing on an airplane, the recommended action during an emergency is to put on your own oxygen mask before helping others. There are two reasons for this: one is that you can't help others if you yourself are unable to breathe, and the other is that terrified people are more willing to put on an ugly oxygen mask if you already have one on. The same goes for your email. You can't help anyone who writes you if you yourself are drowning in email, and you can only train your colleagues how best to work with you if you are using good email habits.

At the risk of losing some friends, try the following experiment. Simultaneously email 10 colleagues a silly question, something akin to, "I can't find the future university calendar list. Do you know what the first day classes will be in the fall of _____?" and see how unbelievably fast some of your colleagues get back to you. Those are busy professors who are not working undisturbed on meaningful life goals but are instead spending their life valuing how many emails they send and receive.

And finally, how many of you have 100, 1,000, or more emails in your inbox? Why on this green Earth would you do that? It isn't like you are going to someday go through all those emails and respond to them. Moreover, too many busy professors use their inbox as their TO DO list. Do not make this mistake. Your email inbox is a terrible TO DO list. If you have more than 1,000 emails in your inbox right now, it is time to declare an email disaster emergency. Stop reading this book, open your email, and drag everything in your inbox into a folder you create called Email Graveyard. I promise you that you will feel so much better if you have zero emails in your inbox, and you can start fresh tomorrow.

Four *Busy Professor* TO DO lists

The most organized *Busy Professors* often have four very simple and easy-to-use TO DO lists: TO DO Today, TO DO in Five Minutes, TO DO Someday, and their Calendar. These lists can be on paper or 3x5 note cards or electronic. I happen to like the simple electronic ones because they can be shared across smart phones, laptops, and desktops (more on using smart phone apps to do this later in the book). Let's briefly consider each of these in turn.

Today's three-item TO DO list. Described in depth earlier, each morning the most productive *Busy Professors* take a quiet moment and decide what their priorities are for the coming day. This means selecting three TO DO items that have meaningful consequences down the road in moving toward tenure, promotion, or toward other important life-work goals.

These should be tasks that require 40-90 minutes' worth of undisturbed attention and directly enhance something on your CV.

A good measure of how important it is might be whether it has an urgent deadline, as things with urgent deadlines rarely are worthwhile things. The late productivity master Stephen Covey, author of the classic text *Seven Habits of Highly Productive People*, would probably counsel us that the key difference between harried busy professors and flourishing *Busy Professors* is that *Busy Professors* distinguish between urgent and important. Urgent items metaphorically scream, "Me first, me first!" while important items whisper.

I haven't tried it myself, by I'm repeatedly advised that this goal-setting works even better at night before going to bed or at the end of the day at your desk, so that you have a clear direction and motivation for hoping out of bed the next morning to begin your day. At the very least, you should keep a notepad and pencil next to your bed in case you wake up in the middle of the night and need to get an idea out of your head, so you can then go back to sleep.

The 5-minute TO DO list. Rather than breathlessly running into class or into a meeting at the last second just as things are starting, *Busy Professors* often arrive at scheduled events early. Or, more often, they find themselves waiting on colleagues to show up on time. Or maybe their transportation schedule is disrupted. Everyone finds themselves with an unexpected 10- or 15-minute period of windfall now and again.

To take advantage of these unexpected gifts of time, *Busy Professors* always have a list of quick, mindless TO DO items that can be handled without considerable mental investment within five minutes or less. Maybe it is a quick note to Mom, a congratulatory email to the Dean, a gentle reminder to a colleague that you're patiently still waiting on a review or some data, or a phone call to building maintenance you've been putting off. Perhaps, surprisingly, you get a quick, good-feeling dopamine-hit to your brain if you strike out three or four TO DO items in rapid succession, even if they don't enhance your CV.

I should be honest and mention that some things on my 5-minute TO DO list take more than 5 minutes, sometimes even up to 20 minutes. And sometimes, items on my 5-minute TO DO list get long and start to reach time-sensitive urgent status (like letters of recommendation. In these cases, I simply make "clean up my 5-minute TO DO list" one of my daily three-item goals. I probably have to do this at least once a week, sometimes more. But the key thing here is that I'm purposefully choosing to spend my time getting these tasks done, rather than having them loom over me as some vague and distracting menace.

The simmering tickle-file TO DO list. We would be naïve if we pretended that all professors do not have a long list of items that they could do, need to do, and want to do. Although Benjamin Franklin warned us long ago that humans need not do all that they can do every day, there are still many, many things that flow through our brains that merit at least a little consideration. I keep a long and ever-growing list of TO DO items—most of which I acknowledge will never actually get done—in a simmering tickle-file. This list is a bit of a kitchen stove top pot of soup that I keep bubbling in the background, just out of my cognitive field of view. Although I probably add to it every day, I only look at it occasionally to tickle my memory.

This long TO DO list includes articles and grant proposals I'd like to write, data I'd like to query, experiments I'd like to run, potential collaborators I'd like to get to know better, and people I should follow up with. I also include in this list non-academic things that come to mind, like books or movies recommended to me. It is the place where I dump things that inevitably flow into my head, interrupting my train of thought when I'm trying to focus on something else. Getting them jotted down and out of my head helps me more quickly return to the task at hand.

The Calendar. Every *Busy Professor* uses a calendar. The calendar is where TO DO items like teach class, attend committee meetings, meet with students, go to the gym, remember to order birthday flowers by this date, and meeting and grant proposal submission deadlines are recorded and sequenced. The *Busy Professor* also uses the calendar as a diary of activity for big tasks that take up slots of time. *Busy Professors* log every activity requiring more than 30 minutes to be entombed in their calendar for later review and reflection. At the end of the week, an honest glance at the calendar makes painfully obvious what your priorities are.

An often-told story about a business executive at a large Fortune 500 company goes something this:

A highly-successful executive was asked to identify what the most important thing in his life was, to which he enthusiastically responded, "My family." However, a review of his calendar revealed late nights in the office working on required reports, extended dinner meetings with potential high-commission clients, and weekend travel. These legitimate, work-related events required him to miss afternoon soccer games, evening school plays, birthday parties, and anniversary dinners. One might reasonably question if his family really is the most important thing in his life, since his time is predominately being spent elsewhere.

Please do not misunderstand my intent here. I'm not making moral judgements in any shape or form; I'm simply giving you the tools you need to escape a frantic academic life and get one that you say you really want. *Busy Professors* who decide to live a life full of scholarly creativity and intellectual engagement really do have to make sure that their calendar includes a good dose of these things that made them want to become a professor in the first place, less they risk becoming one of their unproductive, unfinished TO DO list items and unhappily busy professor colleagues.

<u>*Busy Professor*'s four-list strategy</u>
- ✓ Today's three-item TO DO list
- ✓ The 5-minute TO DO list
- ✓ The simmering, tickle-file TO DO list
- ✓ The Calendar

I should alert you to the fact that successful TO DO list strategies evolve over time, and you would benefit from being open to trying and adapting a number of different approaches to see what works for you. The underlying key here is to be sure that you spend your limited time and limited intellectual energy doing what you deem as being most important, not what someone else's email screams at you as being the most important.

When I first started working in university administration, an important piece of advice I was given from my mentors was,

"Being a great administrator means learning what is mission-critical and which requests you can safely ignore because you never have enough hours to do it all." I pass this same advice to you. You really can do anything you want, but you cannot do everything. You must choose before someone else chooses for you.

The take-away message is simply this: overwhelmed busy professors spend their life trying to whittle down their ever-growing TO DO lists, always adding more items each day than they remove, and becoming emotionally drained by the entire process. In contrast, flourishing *Busy Professors* constantly compare potential TO DO list items with their goals of living the academic life they dreamed of. Moreover, *Busy Professors* aggressively protect their TO DO list from the whirlwind that spins up every day on campus (notoriously disruptive in the afternoon), and only promise themselves they will get done the important items that can be complete without the benefit of good luck or unexpected fortune. *Busy Professors* actively choose to be successful, productive, and happy every day based on what goes on their TO DO lists and to what their scarce resources get applied.

Gotta-Do

TO DO list items should be sufficiently detailed so others can interpret their purpose

Only plan on doing a few items on your TO DO list every day, making certain those items are really important to move forward professionally

Keep things simple and do not waste time creating complicated TO DO systems

Keep a calendar to log accomplished daily activity for review and reflection

---

STEP THREE:
Create a highly-structured syllabus

In this chapter, I am going to reveal two trade secrets of top performing *Busy Professors* that struggling busy professors do not know. The first is how to cover all the topics in your teaching that you need to without cramming everything into the last two weeks of the term. The second secret is how to get great teaching evaluations at the same time. Have I caught your attention? Here is how thriving *Busy Professors* accomplish these seemingly impossible secrets—simultaneously.

Focus your teaching plans on students instead of yourself
　　I want you to imagine for a moment that you suddenly and unexpectedly became ill during the term and were unable to teach for several weeks. Add to this imaginary nightmare scenario your colleagues all being so busy and overly scheduled that they are completely unable to teach your classes for you. Would students in your class be able to still learn, or would everything seize-up, your students consequently losing weeks of learning opportunities? This is a very real situation that unfortunately happens all the time, leaving departments in an awkward lurch. For prospering *Busy Professors* who are so productive and rapidly growing in international renown, such a situation could be actualized when you are invited to give a last minute scholarly lecture tour in Europe during the term.
　　The only way to limit the damage to your students' learning from you unexpectedly being out of the classroom in these unfortunate (or fortunate) events is to adopt wholesale an astonishingly rare teaching philosophy: "It is not what the professor does that matters; it is what the students do."
　　This phrase exemplifies the core idea of a student-centered classroom. When adopting a student-centered teaching philosophy, you remove yourself from being the focus on the

class. Student-centered classrooms are about finding all the ways possible to help and coach students in learning the course concepts.

The first step to adopting a student-centered teaching approach is to make certain that you are no longer the central disseminator of facts. Far too many busy professors spend their class time inefficiently downloading information to students, usually in lecture form. Lectures are emblematic of professor-centered classrooms, where the professor is the most important source of all information. In such classrooms, professors might have textbooks, but students do not buy them because the professor tells students all they need to know. I've even watched too many professors literally read the textbook to their students. In this case, the professors think of themselves as being so centrally critical to students' learning that students are not actually required to study the assigned textbook readings outside of class, because the professors themselves provide everything that is important—usually doing so by stating that poorly-motivated students never read or can successfully read the textbook anyway. Moreover, in professor-centered classrooms, students do not really need to attend class because they can get everything they need for the exam from their friend's carefully created notes or by getting a detailed exam review sheet from you before the exam.

Before you cast such a situation off as being silly and inapplicable to you, understand that most professor-centered professors do not actually know that they are professor-centered teachers. Was attendance in your class nearly 100% all week this week? (If yes, would you have nearly 100% attendance if you didn't require attendance and make it count as part of their grade?). What if I told you there was a better way? And what if I told you I could simultaneously get you even better teaching evaluations?

In stark contrast to professor-centered classrooms, student-centered classrooms are carefully designed to make sure that the professor is not the only source of information for learning the course material. Courses designed to be student-centered rely heavily on carefully delineated textbook readings; professor-created reading guides highlighting what students should notice when they read; frequent homework exercises that allow students to further engage and practice using an idea in novel situations; collaborative classroom-activities where students socially engage with one another to become better able to explain, extend, and apply class topics; critically selected online videos; grade-independent practice quizzes; and examinations and projects that are tightly and explicitly aligned with the preceding list of learning activities. Student-centered classes designed in this way use the professor as a motivational coach, a critical tour guide, an occasional story teller, a learning leader, and most importantly, a source of meaningful feedback for students' depth of learning.

The bottom line here is that only a student-centered course like this can survive you spending a month in Europe or of unexpectedly falling ill. But here is the great surprise: *Busy Professors* who carefully design courses to be about the student learning experience get far better course evaluations than busy professors who make the course all about themselves—more on this later.

Provide students with a daily schedule for the entire term...*and stick to it*

Novice learners—your students—depend on you to have sufficient knowledge of the course content and its structure to build a clear and easy-to-follow pathway to successfully learning the course material. Students have little idea what actual learning material in your specific discipline looks like. Should your students be highlighting their course textbook and making flash cards for memorization? Should your students be working problems in the back of the book and even making up problems of their own to swap with classmates? Should your students be seeking out and listening to lectures from other scholars in your domain? Should students read the assigned readings twice and critically challenge the conclusions the author is drawing? It certainly isn't all these things, because different disciplines require different learning activities from their students. Physics professors clearly do not want their students to compose philosophical essays on why their textbook author is incorrect, whereas literature professors sometimes do! Your students do not know what people in your discipline do to engage and learn, so they need you to help them participate in those specific activities.

At the same time, students have no idea how fast to be moving through the material. Some professors seem to have given little thought to how fast they should be moving through the material, as evidenced by how many busy professors tell me at the end of the term that they are madly rushing their lectures to get through all the concepts that they had planned or are required to cover.

Given that preamble, *Busy Professors* who are highly successful and prepared purposefully build for students—and themselves—a detailed daily schedule of course learning activities, distribute it to students, and refer to it frequently with their students during class and by themselves. As a result, they and their students are committed to sticking to the schedule no matter what happens during scheduled class time.

Imagine a syllabus that includes a five-column table where each row is a class-meeting day. The columns going from right to left are labeled: | Class Date | Before Class | During Class | After Class | Notes |. You might also benefit from adding a column for "topic" or one for a guiding "focus question" such as, "How is starlight generated?" A syllabus schedule that really works is sufficiently detailed; not only should an unexpected substitute professor be able to pick it up and use it in your absence, but learning pathway students could follow it in the absence of an instructional leader.

Busy Professors always make a detailed learning plan for students and themselves to follow, and religiously stick to it even when scheduled class time doesn't go as planned, or for some unanticipated reason (like inclement weather or worse), class gets canceled. This keeps *Busy Professors'* courses and their teaching under control and out of the crazy-making whirlwind that inevitably happens at universities, causing frantic busy professors to crumble and endlessly complain. Sound like a lot of work? It is…but there are other benefits to a highly structured, student-centered syllabus.

The Busy Professor

Class Date	Before Class	During Class	After Class	Notes
Nov 9	Read pp. 318-341	Complete mini-case study 11	HW 11: items 1-16	Check out YouTube https://youtu.be/X36p when stuck
Nov 11	Pre-reading task 12	Review ideas supporting uniformitarianism	Review scores on HW 10	Compare your 1st half of HW 11 answers with another student's
Nov 13	Read pp. 341-363	Create practice-test questions in groups	Re-read pp. 318-341	Start preparing for end of next week's exam by re-reading assigned readings
Nov 16	Re-read pp. 318-341	Complete and review ungraded practice quiz answers	HW 11: items 16-25 & submit all HW 11	Re-copy your class notes from last week and create your study-review package as described in the syllabus

Leverage your structured syllabus into better teaching evaluations

Busy Professors are committed to both creating a solid, easy-to-follow learning pathway for their students and abiding by it themselves throughout the term. One of the side benefits turns out to be higher scoring end-of-term course evaluations from students.

At the end of nearly every term, most universities require students to complete end-of-term course evaluations about the courses they have just taken. Much berated by faculty across the planet for both valid and invalid reasons, end-of-term course evaluations are a reality of teaching in higher education. As it turns out, students are also exhausted by filling out end-of-term course evaluations for all their different classes. Imagine if you are a student and during the last week of the term, you're required to fill out five or six of these forms for all your professors. Moreover, the end-of-term course evaluation forms sometimes vary significantly from department to department, applying an additional cognitive tax on students trying to complete these forms who are already tired at the end of a term. To add insult to injury, students know that the lousy professor they have for their least favorite class probably received terrible reviews from students last year, and those reviews didn't make any difference, so why take this year's meaningless review seriously either?

In response, interviews with students reveal that students stop reading the carefully constructed prompts and simply respond to two overarching ideas, regardless of what the item specifically asks: (*i*) was the professor authentically interested in me being successful in the class, and (*ii*) did the professor create and follow an easy-to-follow pathway for me to master the course content.

What we've learned here is simply this: when *Busy Professors* build a student-centered course and promote a clear pathway for student success, higher student evaluation scores will follow. And when coupled with the repeated notion from the opening chapter that structure allows freedom, taking time to create a highly structured syllabus is a win-win for *Busy Professors* everywhere.

Use a routine to add teaching innovations

Each year, discipline-based education research is providing more and more specific direction on how universities can design and deliver more successful instruction and help a wider diversity of students achieve higher levels of learning. At the same time, a visit to most teaching-excellence workshops will provide professors with far too many innovative teaching tools and intellectual engagement techniques to be implemented during any single semester. In fact, the most common question I get at any teaching excellence workshop is about how to implement all the great teaching tools available. The answer for *Busy Professors* is to not implement everything but schedule only a single new idea or two each semester.

When parents teach their kids how to clean house, the mantra is "everything in its place." *Busy Professors* need a similar mantra for implementing teaching innovations and the many time-saving productivity ideas that are covered in this book. *Busy Professors* schedule a time for everything, including implementation of new ideas.

<u>*Busy Professor's* every Monday strategy</u>
If you want to implement a new strategy, commit to...
- ✓ Every Monday, I will assign students a pre-class question
- ✓ Every Wednesday, I will do one new collaborative activity
- ✓ Every Thursday afternoon, I'll work somewhere outside my building
- ✓ Every Friday afternoon, I will deal with any backed-up email.
- ✓ One day each month, I will reconsider the list of next 10 titles I'm going to write

If you want to start distributing to students a pre-class question they are to answer before arriving to class, then this needs to be regularly scheduled; you can commit for this to occur every Monday by scheduling time on your calendar to create and distribute a new question every Friday. By the end of the term, you will have 10 to 15 new questions to use again next year.

If you want to have students answer collaborative questions in class more often, you must rigorously schedule when you are going to pose collaborative questions in class. For example, you might schedule showing up to class every Wednesday with some pre-prepared questions for students to answer in small, collaborative learning groups. Again, by the end of the term, you will have 10 to 15 new question sets to use again next year, and if you add doing it on Fridays as well next year, you'll double the number of question sets you will have for the following years.

The same goes for making time to read more journal articles, to experiment in the laboratory on a side project, or spend more time collaborating with colleagues. Scheduling these tasks gives you more freedom to do what you want instead of letting the academic whirlwind catch you and dash you against the rocks. You simply have to know what you want, and make it happen. Just like you will rarely "feel" like going to the gym, you will never "find" time for these important things to happen.

Instead, *Busy Professors* "make" time for these important things to happen.

Gotta-Do

Change your class from being all about you to becoming student-centered instead so it can largely operate without you

Add to your syllabus a daily schedule that includes specific directions for what students should be doing before and after class, and which indicates what you will be doing during class to coach learning and provide meaningful feedback to students

Share with students an easy-to-follow learning pathway to being successful in your class

Regularly schedule the implementation of innovative teaching ideas

---

STEP FOUR:
Don't break your writing appointments

When constantly comparing a happily producing *Busy Professor*'s life with an unhappily overwhelmed busy professor's life, I might have mistakenly given you the impression that busy professors are lazy people, or that somehow, they are not dedicated to their jobs. This is not my intention, and nothing could be farther from the truth. In fact, I would suggest it is quite the opposite.

My sense is that the majority of busy professors are incredibly busy with the minutia of their jobs, striving to ensure that everything that can be done gets done. They work early in the morning, they work late into the evenings, they work on weekends, and they even work during vacations, if they take them. Moreover, because many of the busiest professors can easily point to a long list of completed tasks following in the wake behind them and a long list of will-certainly-get-done tasks coming up on their horizon, they might even be quite happy and generally satisfied with their lives overall by seeing value in the sheer volume they have accomplished.

What I am pointing out here is that *Busy Professors* you want to emulate actively plan their lives and spend their scarce time purposefully, whereas the unifying characteristic of busy professors is that they are reactive and most often choose to do whatever task is most urgently in front of them. With the best of intentions, my experience is that both kinds of professors do set aside time in their calendars for important tasks without deadlines, such as reading in the library, writing grant proposals, or reviewing instructional materials to improve next year's class. What is different is that when scheduled, *Busy Professors* always choose to do what is important, rather than what is urgent or screaming loudest for attention. And there is always something urgent begging for your attention.

Don't break your writing appointments

Imagine for a moment that in your calendar you've allocated Friday mornings from 9-10:30 am for undisturbed creative writing in a nearby coffee shop. You know this is a reasonably good time choice because many of your colleagues are teaching in this time band, so the chances you will be asked to attend a department meeting are reduced. What will you do if the department chair requests for you to attend a college budget meeting during this time? What will you do if a student begs if they can meet you during this time for help on a homework assignment? Unquestionably, this situation challenges the very core of what it means to be a professor who really does have the privilege of being able to choose how to spend their time each day.

When I pose this very real quandary to professors in my *Busy Professor* time management and productivity workshops, the most immediate response is to acquiesce to the request—just this once—and move the allocated writing time to another slot in the calendar. Such a solution seems reasonable on the surface.

However, just to be certain we are considering all possibilities, what if you did not have writing on your schedule during that time slot, but instead were teaching? Would you cancel your scheduled class so that you could attend a budget meeting or meet with a struggling student? Of course not. There is really no decision here—you would say, "I'm sorry, I'm teaching during that time" and no one would question you.

In this case, you've made a value judgement that teaching is the most important thing on your calendar. One can reasonably argue that scheduled teaching slots are immovable and writing slots are flexible and can be easily rescheduled. While this is true in theory, what happens in practice is that a non-CV building activity replaces a CV building activity and that writing time gets lost in the whirlwind of academia and never replaced—or worse, replaces evening or weekend time when you should be healing yourself and enjoying the other half of work-life balance. If you want to live a balanced life and have spent your limited time doing what you think is important, then don't break your writing appointments.

In the end, there is a far more important reason to schedule and keep regular writing appointments with yourself.

Many professors really struggle to get words down on a blank page. It has been suggested that academic writing most often looks like, "Write four paragraphs, erase three, and declare victory." Regardless if this is true or not, what is definitely true is that the more you write, the easier it becomes. People that write just a little every day end up being able to write more words per day in a very short time frame than people who do not. Moreover, the research is clear that the act of writing stimulates even more ideas in your head. The result is that the more you try to write, the faster you become, and best of all, the more you write, the more ideas of what to write about will pop into your head. *Busy Professors* that make sure they write at least 1,000 words each morning end up with an overflowing well of ideas to write about, which they will never have enough time to get around to. In other words, the simple act of writing causes your brain to generate ideas. If you find yourself having nothing to write about, and a daily journaling regime doesn't get you unstuck in just a few weeks, find a prolific *Busy Professor* who will partner with you, because they have plenty to write about and ideas to share for collaborative writing.

Use your calendar as your navigational logbook

I find the concept of accurately sailing across the ocean from point to point, far from land, a simultaneously fascinating and terrifying concept. A ship's navigator has the life-and-death task of keeping track of a ship's location based largely on where it has been and where it is going. Traditionally, these records of where a ship has been and how fast it has been moving was kept in a *logbook*. A logbook gets its name from the wooden logs or wood chips ancient mariners would toss off the back of their boats. The wood was attached to a rope that had pretied knots at regular intervals, and sailors would count how many knots passed through their hands as the ship sailed away from the floating log to determine the ship's speed, thus carefully measuring its distance from its last known position. The logbook is critical in all of navigation because if you do not know where you have been, it is impossible to figure out where you are going.

A *Busy Professor*'s logbook is the real-time data and evidence needed to reflect on how their day-to-day, week-to-week academic life is going. Whereas an annual CV update or annual performance review lists solid, summative milestones like number of pages published, number of journal articles reviewed, and amount of extramural grant dollars awarded, it provides scant formative information that is immediately actionable.

Imagine serving as a department head and formally informing a junior third-year assistant professor they need to publish more and do less service if they want to be promoted someday. For an unmentored novice faculty member, this crushing news is usually interpreted simply as, "Work harder and work more hours." This interpretation is mostly meaningless. Given that there are only 24 hours in a day, the best solution here is to help that junior academic understand which time-consuming activities are helping them move toward building a promotable CV, which time-consuming activities are interfering, and respond accordingly. This can only be done if there is logbook data available.

Busy Professors use their calendar—electronic or paper-based—as both their planner and their logbook. As a planner, the *Busy Professor*'s calendar provides a reliable and easy-to-use tool for hard scheduling *Gotta-do* tasks, like teaching classes, going to the gym, hosting collaborative group meetings, unavoidable committee meetings, and deadlines for conference and grant proposals. As a tool for collecting day-to-day activity data, the *Busy Professor*'s calendar provides a reliable and easy-to-use diary for reflection and reassessment.

When learning how to better manage money, the first task money mentors give to their clients is to carefully track every penny one spends for a week. The consistent result is that people are amazed, even shocked, at where their money went. The initial goal of most improved money management programs is to build an individual's awareness of where their limited money goes so that they can start to make rational decisions about a scarce resource.

The same is true for mentoring professors about time management. If you track how you spend every minute for a week, you will likely be astounded where you spent your limited time. The thinking here is the same: if you are fully cognizant of how you are spending your minutes every day, then you can make more rational decisions about how to move forward professionally. Invest your time in things that really matter and avoid those time-sinks that quietly suck away your time, giving nothing in return. Your calendar is the best way to purposefully plan your time and gather information for later reflection about making changes to your academic life. *Busy Professors* keep their calendar within reach and log every activity in 30-minute or 60-minute blocks and review it weekly.

Batch everything... *stop multitasking*

After apathy and lack of basic reading, (*w*)riting, and (*a*)rithmetic skills, the next biggest complaint I hear from faculty is that students mistakenly believe they can multitask. This detrimental multitasking shows up as students use their smart phones during class, watch television while doing homework, or chat with friends while completing reading assignments. It seems that no matter what you tell students, or show them the research, or even do simple, objective demonstrations with them, nothing dissuades students hellbent on multitasking to *stop* multitasking. As it turns out, the same seems to go for their hypocritical professors who cannot multitask either.

A quick, personal story: when our youngest kids started doing the dishes unsupervised, we noticed that the relatively simple, previously practiced-with-an-adult task would take them an inordinately long period of time to complete. When we watched them, we were surprised to see that their dish washing strategy was to: [1.] wash one single dish; [2.] rinse one single dish; and [3.] towel dry that single dish, then repeat the process. This linear approach makes some theoretical sense, but from a practical point of view takes forever to complete!

Similarly, we were watching with a group of novice astronomy students at the telescope observatory—where nighttime hours with clear, dark skies are few and precious—and these students would record an observation, then take ten minutes to complete some data analysis while the awaiting telescope stood by unused, before making another observation. The result of their approach was that the telescope remained unused most of the available evening.

To make my point even more vigorously, you might have seen—or even been—the professor who has a giant stack of homework assignments sitting on the desk waiting to be graded. For some, this is depressing. Imagine if the professor's strategy was to grade a paper or two, then turn to their email to send off a quick note, then grade a paper or two before being interrupted by a text message exchange with a colleague…then grade a paper or two before getting up to go refill the awaiting coffee cup. Using this approach, the stack of papers is going to take all day, and perhaps into the night, to get processed. Hard to imagine, but I've witnessed this time and time again.

What do all these scenarios have in common? *Busy Professors* get more things done because they choose to do what busy professors do not. In this case, *Busy Professors* make plans to collect and complete their similar tasks together in one big batch. They wash all the dishes before rising all the dishes. They make all their scientific measurements before doing the analysis tasks that do not require the scarce instrument time. And they grade all their papers before being distracted away and doing something else.

There are three solid reasons that *Busy Professors* batch everything. The first reason is that multitasking does not work. Period. One cannot do a complete job on a task and even have a chance to enjoy it if they are busy thinking about something else. The second reason is that batching tasks accomplishes everything quicker. Finishing tasks quicker is important to *Busy Professors* who have other things they want to do. Third, needless task-switching consumes cognitive energy. Because sending smart phone text messages uses a different part of your brain than grading papers, switching between tasks needlessly wastes your scarce mental energy that could be applied to other intellectual pursuits.

I know this chapter has gone on quite a while—but I believe getting your academic life under control is required to enjoy the academic life you have worked so hard to get. You are going to use email—so batch all your email time together and do not let it dribble away your energy and your time. You have places to be and things to do at specific times, so use your calendar to plan your time and be sure to put items in your calendar that really matter to you. By adopting a highly structured approach to your day, you can get what needs to be done finished, so you have the freedom to enjoy your academic and non-academic life. The overriding principle that *Busy Professors* are striving for is to keep "the main thing, the main thing," whatever that happens to be. To accomplish their goals, *Busy Professors* use a calendar and abhor multitasking.

Gotta-Do

Get a calendar and use it to clearly mark time to do the things you must do and the things you want to do

Use your calendar as a diary to reflect on whether you are spending your limited time on what is important rather than what seems urgent

Don't break your regular writing appointments, because the act of writing generates new ideas

Avoid multitasking by batching similar tasks—like email processing—together on your calendar

---

STEP FIVE:
Automate everything

Last century's golden promise that the invention of computers and ubiquity of the Internet would make work easier and save us time, thus leading us ever closer to a happy life of leisure, hasn't quite panned out like we hoped. Sure, we can do things faster. But for far too many unhappy busy professors, faster only means we end up being able to do more things that fail to bring us happiness. If those "things" aren't the things that bring us unbridled joy, what does it really matter if we can simply do more of the things that are just *things* in less time than it took before? More of a thing is not necessarily better, it is just more.

There are, however, a great many things that computers and the Internet can do for us better than we can that can be a great benefit to a *Busy Professor*'s productivity level and overall happiness. These are related to the world of automation, where the computer systems of the world do it for you. *Busy Professors* stop what they are doing and make the time required to set up their world so as much as possible is automated for them.

Automate your grading

Multiple-choice exams are common practice in many college courses, and there are countless strategies lying around about how to speed up the processes of writing, scoring, and recording student performance. One of the most common strategies used to grade faster entails using a removable front-page answer sheet where students' record their responses, and a corresponding answer-key with holes punched out to speed grading for rapid hand-marking. The most common strategy for easing the burden of writing new multiple-choice questions each time has been to retain students' exams without allowing students to take copies of the test from the exam room so that exams can be reused.

Most professors are aware of the existence of scanning technology, where students use a No. 2 lead pencil to mark bubbles on a scannable answer sheet. However, most departments are too small to have one. You might be surprised to learn that there is probably one hidden somewhere on your campus, should you be able find and use it. When using this approach, it is critical to know precisely which scannable bubble form students should be using, as they are highly specific. Most commonly, students can obtain them at the campus bookstore.

In recent years, the traditional paper-and-pencil approach to testing is being replaced by Internet-delivered computer systems, usually in the form of CMS Course Management Systems or LMS Learning Management Systems, paid for by the college. These systems have many useless bells and whistles, but what they do provide is rock-solid secure quiz and testing systems. Faculty woefully underutilize these handy, time-saving tools. These systems automatically grade students' answers, inform students of their scores, and enter that information into a secure grade book. By far the most time-consuming part is entering in questions and correctly keyed answers, but the payoff on the backend is incredible.

These systems also allow students to submit short- or long-answer essay-style responses securely. Students do this work in the traditional classroom, if required, by bringing their laptops, tablets, or smart phones to class—which nearly all students have. In the theoretical event they do not have such a tool, you can help them make arrangements to work in the library or computer lab, or even allow them to write on traditional paper, but I've never had it actually happen. And once you are paper-less, then providing typed feedback on your part becomes a million times easier.

Of course, there are many great subscription-based Internet grading systems, and if I were to describe and review them in any detail here, there would be new, improved ones replacing the old, still-working ones before I could even finish this chapter. There are systems that look for grammar, systems that check for plagiarism, and ones that provide smart-feedback depending on students' responses. There are newer and better and cheaper ones showing up every semester, and you probably receive plenty of marketing materials about them. They really are totally worth the set-up time at the beginning of the term, as they are largely a set-it-up-and-forget-it system. Personally, I think the more students submit work and the more feedback they get, the more they will learn, and the more you can focus on the less mechanical parts of your job.

Automate your investing

When you started your job, you might have had a brief orientation about your benefits, such as health insurance and retirement. Likely, those meetings are long-forgotten in the haze of a starting a new position. Whereas busy professors just hope things will work out and perhaps slowly run up giant credit card bills, *Busy Professor*s have purposeful systems in place to manage their finances, and, in particular, retirement savings. You might also be interested in saving for an important goal, like buying a house, going on a very special vacation, life insurance premiums, putting away money for a child's college fund, or maybe even just enough to buy some holiday gifts next December without going into debt.

When I was younger, banks had what they called "Christmas Club Accounts" where, starting in February, they would automatically take $10 out of your paycheck on payday and place it in a special account. Then, 10 months later in November, you magically had $100 for holiday gift-giving. The realization that $10 each month is hardly noticeable but $100 is a tremendous amount of magically-appearing money is key to making sure you have a secure financial future.

Busy Professors use this automated magic to take care of everything. You can easily set up with your bank's online system to automatically move tiny amounts of money into a specially designated savings account every payday. This is further important because you can save money on insurance and other big-ticket items if you pay once annually instead of monthly or quarterly. I have tons of individual accounts I contribute a small amount to each month, so I can stay as far away from evil, unforgiving, high-interest credit cards as possible.

<u>*Busy Professor*'s Separate Monthly Savings Account Examples</u>
- ✓ Emergencies
- ✓ Taxes
- ✓ Extra-Retirement
- ✓ Holiday gift-giving
- ✓ Car license, taxes, & auto insurance
- ✓ Anticipated auto repair
- ✓ Annual life insurance
- ✓ Vacation & travel

Busy Professors often find themselves unexpectedly enhancing their incomes by doing consulting, earning published book royalties, and receiving honoraria for speaking or winning prizes. Usually, these extra winnings have unexpected income tax implications, and wise *Busy Professors* dutifully place 25% of their windfalls into a dedicated savings account to pay any unexpected tax-bills showing up each April. *Busy Professors* take full advantage of the compounding Christmas Club Account effect and put a little away each month so that there are no surprises down the road.

Automate paying your bills

Busy Professors have a plethora of intellectually stimulating things they want to do during the year. Little distractions here and there unremittingly drain one's cognitive attention drip by drip. One of those nagging little things is the stack of monthly bills. We're talking about the mortgage, rent, car payment, student loan payment, electricity, gas, water, Netflix, cell phone, insurance, and on and on and on, all of which require energy to be maintained.

Busy Professors set up their lives so that their monthly bills get paid automatically. If you are disciplined enough to pay 100% of the debt each month, this is a fantastic way to earn a tremendous number of credit card benefit points, like airline frequent flier miles or hotel points. If you are inclined even the tiniest bit to let a credit card balance accumulate, then using your bank's free online bill pay service to pay them directly from your primary checking account at the beginning of each month is the way to go. Don't forget to set up all your credit cards to automatically deduct the minimum payment required each month from your bank account, so that you never ever have a late payment. Taking time to set this up is critical if you want to focus on living your life, because these monthly annoyances really mount up, sucking the life right out of you.

Automate your social media postings

Personally, I am torn about the importance social media should play in your professional life. I am not torn, however, about the role of social media in our *personal* life. There is absolutely no place for social media in your personal life. The tiny bit of good out there, like seeing updated pictures of your grandchildren, is far overshadowed by the negative aurora-consuming social media. Scholarly work by Martin Seligman and others shows that people feel depressed after looking at social media, either because they see happy people who seem happier than they are, or they see unhappy people and feel empathy for them unnecessarily. The rapidly growing research based on happiness is rather clear. Happiness comes from ongoing relationships, extended engagement in projects, and meaningful purpose that comes from serving causes bigger than ourselves—and absolutely none of this happens in the cesspool of social media.

Professionally, there are perhaps some benefits to being on social media, mostly in the realm of self-promotion. We haven't talked about self-promotion much here because academics generally shun self-promotion, even though academics seem to engage in the practice frequently. There is a mythical illusion that academia is a meritocracy, and that the people doing the best work should automatically rise to the top of notoriety. The pathway that this false narrative recommends is for professors to downplay, or even loudly mention, one's professional successes. This make-believe storyline is complete baloney, as nothing could be farther from the truth. *Busy Professors* strive to do good work, and they do not hide that good work from their colleagues, even though jealousy is certain to arise in the most surprising of corners. Social media is one way that *Busy Professors* should distribute the results of their work—because you won't be invited to give conference lectures or be nominated for academic awards if people do not know of your work and having at least some online presence is required these days for this to occur.

So how does a *Busy Professor* utilize social media to self-promote one's good works without getting sucked into the vortex of the worst of social media? If you are self-disciplined, one solution is to post and schedule future posts without reading anyone else's social media posts. If you are still building up your self-discipline, then the best solution is to quickly search the Internet for "simultaneous posting to social media at once" and you will be presented with numerous web-based programs that will simultaneously post or post items as scheduled for you. For example, I work with a team that distributes a quarterly email newsletter of upcoming events and opportunities for academics. My task on the team is to take those newsletter items and ensure that one gets inserted into the social media stream each week, so that people visiting the group's Facebook page see what looks like an active online presence. It takes about 30 minutes to set up the next three months of scheduled postings, and our group can be "present" in social media without any one of us personally getting sucked into that inescapable social media black hole. The same goes for blogging. Academics can temporarily post their budding academic ideas and get interactive feedback faster than from a traditional journal, which only works if blogging is a temporary tool to advance one's intellectual thinking. Blogging is never the core focus activity of *Busy Professors* and certainly never the end-product.

This approach of scheduling automated social media posting has the additional benefit of keeping *Busy Professors* out of the rapid response mistake. Far too many of my busy professor colleagues are too busy reading and posting and reading and replying and reading and posting again to publish anything because they have become inflamed about an issue of the moment, brought to their attention by the tsunami or the 24-hour news cycle news-alerts. Remember that no matter how eloquent a social media response is, no one ever has their political mind fundamentally changed because of what they read posted on social media. Social media is specially designed to be a den of confirmation bias that serves only to construct easily identifiable, large-scale commercial demographic markets. Because they know this, *Busy Professors* keep their focus on the production of archival level scholarship instead of engaging in quickly evaporating 240-character social media spars or buried, rarely read, blog posts.

Automate your exercise

I know you are excited to learn about how to use the computer to automate your exercise, so you no longer have to go to the gym. I myself seem to have allergic-like reactions when I go to the gym—I get short of breath, my blood pressure and pulse go up, and I break into a sweat—all signs of an allergic reaction, I'm certain. Unfortunately, to be honest, we can't automate the actual physical activity at the gym, but computers, gym equipment, and the Internet can make exercise seem easier.

There are three aspects to going to the gym. The first aspect is make the disciplined decision to join the gym and make (not find) time to go. As is so often the case, busy professors believe they are far too busy doing stuff to do what is required to help their physical bodies support the exhausting mental work required of creative *Busy Professors*. The most difficult thing about a gym workout is getting to the gym, so if you can just get make yourself walk inside the door, your workout is nearly finished! Some people find they are better able to get to the gym if they have a workout buddy whom they don't want to let down by skipping their gym-date.

The second aspect is that you need a workout plan that you just do without having to think about it. Cardio-machines like the elliptical are perfect for automated aerobic exercise, as those computerized machines do all the thinking, adjusting, and monitoring for you. If weight training is more your style (eventually you should do both cardio and weight training), then cycling through the entire row of weight machines is easy enough. Again, *Busy Professors* make time to do this because they know that increased exercise makes the brain more cognitively sharp, deeply creative, and mentally focused. Just forty minutes five times each week works amazingly well.

The third aspect is that you need headphones and a distraction. Now, I fully realize that we've spent thousands of words discussing strategies and tactics for you to eliminate distractions in your life so that you can do the work of the *Busy Professor*, so my recommendation for finding a distraction might seem odd. However, distracting yourself with binging Netflix or YouTube on the elliptical, or listening to audiobooks while using weight machines, makes the time fly by faster. Moreover, if you strictly limit yourself to only watching your favorite Netflix series while you are in the gym, then you have something to look forward to doing while at the gym, which can provide that extra needed motivation to get there.

The caveat here with automated exercise is that fitness instructors clearly know that lifting and balancing free-weights is more effective than some complex weight machine with pre-determined resistances, and that purposeful swimming is far better than a bells and whistles cardio-machine with a video screen. However, we all know that any exercise you do is far better than not exercising at all. If you need to use the machines and Netflix, Hulu, Amazon-Prime, YouTube, and ESPN-style distractions to effortlessly work your physique in the service of more creative brain activity, then by all means, do automated exercise.

Busy Professors make an extra effort to be sure that real exercise plans show up in their calendars. Research clearly shows that your brain just works better when your body gets exercise, and *Busy Professors* need their brains to work so that they can enjoy the intellectual part of being an academic.

Gotta-Do

Automate grading by using paper-free homework systems

Automate investing by setting up monthly deposits into dedicated savings accounts

Automate monthly bill-paying activities using a bank's online bill-paying system

Automate social media engagement and avoid day-to-day post and reply cycle

Automate your exercise to keep your brain in a creative work mode

STEP SIX:
Put 20-seconds between you and your vice

All academics struggle with things that keep them from doing their job. Even the most devout *Busy Professors* have vices that interfere with being the best *Busy Professors* possible. Sometimes it is the siren call of the latest Netflix show to be binged. Sometimes it is the desire to get a quick dopamine hit from responding to a recently received email so that they can feel like they have accomplished something. Sometimes it is the need to check out social media to try to feel better connected to friends and family. Everyone struggles with these, and you need ready-to-deploy strategies to get back on the *Busy Professor* plan when you've fallen off. Remember not to be too hard on yourself when this occurs, as lapses happen to everyone. Simply acknowledge what happened and get back on the program doing what you really want to be doing to meet your long-term goals.

20 seconds is all you need

Like everyone else, *Busy Professors* also have a natural desire to simply be lazy. Who wouldn't rather lie snuggling in a warm bed than get up? Who wouldn't rather spend the evening binging the latest new television series? Who wouldn't rather eat ice cream than a warm spinach salad? But there is a tactical solution. If you can put off making your vice come alive by making it more difficult to get to by just 20 seconds, then you can make a better decision.

Twenty seconds feels like an eternity. How long does it take for your laptop computer to start up from full shut-down? How long does it take for a large PDF file to download to your computer from an email? How long does it take to look up a friend's phone number rather than call it from your smart phone's favorite's list? How long does it take for your smart phone to power-up from the "off" setting? These are universally frustrating things that cause humans undue grief when we must wait or dedicate 20 seconds to make something happen. Fortunately, *Busy Professors* can take full advantage of our inherent laziness to keep us away from our vices by building the tiniest of barriers.

Want to watch less TV? Simply remove the batteries from your remote control. You will be amazed how little you will be willing to change the channel during commercials, or even turn the unit on when you have to devote 20 seconds to inserting the batteries.

Want to check your email less often? Simply remove the saved password or desktop shortcut to your email. It only takes a few seconds to enter your password each time you want to check your email on your smart phone or computer, but those precious seconds are all you need to activate the *Busy Professor*'s laziness characteristic, and you will think twice before reading your email.

Want to practice the ukulele more often? Place your ukulele in front of your television, squarely in your field of view from the couch. You will be amazed how often you choose to play your ukulele rather than take effort to move it out of the line of sight to your television.

Want to absently pick up your smart phone less often? Keep your smart phone on a charger out of reach and at a chair-less location where you would physically have to stand up to use it. Same goes for your bedroom; be sure your smart phone charging cable cannot reach the bed, so you will be forced to get out of bed to use it or to shut off the morning wake-up alarm.

Want fewer cell phone interruptions? Power down your phone during a predetermined time frame each day. The eternally long 20 seconds it takes to power on your phone will make a difference. Additionally, turn off the notifications letting you know when you get a text message or an email. Don't worry, if something urgent happens, someone will find you: twenty years ago, none of us had smart phones and we still managed to find one another when needed.

Getting unstuck

Some mornings, I just don't feel like doing anything. We all have those moments where we just can't seem to start working on anything meaningful. How does one get started from full-stop? That's the instant where you've got to close your eyes and commit to just pressing the START button if you want to get going on the day. Once you get going, it is easier to keep moving.

For me, I love snorkeling. Watching colorful fish swim among coral reefs makes me unapologetically grateful for the beauty of this Earth. However, it takes tremendous dedication to dive into that initially cold water, which my body happily adjusts to in just a few seconds. Same goes for me about getting in a cold shower. Sometimes you must screw up the courage to enact sheer will to get started on something.

Commit to just 20 minutes. When I really don't want to get going on something, I tell myself I'll suck it up and work on it for just 20 minutes. Often, that is enough to get the ball rolling, and I find that an hour later I'm still working on the task. This only works if you have your email and smart phone notifications off, because those are the moments your brain is looking for any excuse not to work on the task at hand.

Just open the file. Sometimes, if you can muster energy to open a fresh document, it is enough to get going. This works particularly well when I have something I'm doing with a smart phone app, like meditation, for example. If I can just open the app and start the program or the timer, then I'm able to get moving.

Pomodoro technique. Many of my colleagues love using the *Pomodoro technique*. Named for the tomato-shaped Pomodoro kitchen timer that moderates this approach, the strategy here is to only work on a task for 25 minutes at the most, then stop for at least five minutes. My version of this when working at home is to have a list of 5-minute home tasks—make my bed, start laundry, flip between washer and dryer, match lost sock pairs, start dishwasher, unload dishwasher, take out trash in every room, light vacuum one single room—and stop every half-hour and do just one and only one of these quick tasks to restart my brain. This approach helps me avoid the tendency to deep clean the entire house all day long to keep from doing some work-related tasks I'm just not in the mood to do. At the end of the day, I have both a list of house chores completed and finished my work-related responsibilities. Moreover, I also have a neatly made bed with no dirty clothes on the floor before bedtime, which is an exquisite feeling to have at the end of a productive day.

Keep a time diary. I find that logging my work—writing down the start time and the end time for each micro-task—gets me started and keeps me moving. For this book project specifically, I keep an updated *.xls* spreadsheet with dates, daily written word counts, and total minutes dedicated to the project.

DATE	ACTIONS	TIME	START	END	TOTAL =
2-Feb	set up book.doc, created XLS tracking, created TOC, & wrote 1 pargraph of intro	75	0	577	577
3-Feb	avoid temptation to res. or find pix just focused on getting undedited chp 1 words dow	85	577	1475	898
4-Feb	order cover design, edited pages 3-5, started freedom from structure	70	1475	2322	847
5-Feb	finished chapter one, added random thoughts to preface, avoided editing mode	100	2322	4068	1746
6-Feb	outlining email chapter, rough out preface, found quotes to use in book	65	4068	5820	1752
7-Feb	opening of email chapter, now ready for real gotta try it strategies (2 30 min. sessions)	55	5820	7202	1382
8-Feb	how to email with students, levels of disconnection from email	53	7202	8177	975
9-Feb	finished the email chapter completely, while at the airport (got here 2 hrs early on purp	101	8177	9783	1606
10-Feb	just a little time spent on TO DO lists before family woke up	30	9783	10240	457
11-Feb	purposefully slept late, spent morning with family, was a good trade off	0	0	0	0
12-Feb	after redesigning chp 2 outline, wrote it in one sitting, without distraction	143	10240	12476	2236
13-Feb	outline step 3 (chp 4) and wrote it entirely as I waited for my family to finish their morr	127	12476	15173	2697
14-Feb	wrote most of step 4 (chp 5), need ending, and need better adjectives next time	68	15173	16556	1383
15-Feb	emailed a .doc backup to gmail; talked to cover guy, kept writing, finished step 4	74	16556	18011	1455
16-Feb	stopped by Starbucks for an hour when driving home from airport after all night flight	56	18011	19086	1075
17-Feb	didn't realy want to write today, but forced myself to open the xls, and that got me goi	79	19086	19998	912
18-Feb	automate gym sect., outline 20-second barrier chapter, add books to ref list, email edit	56	19998	21177	1179
19-Feb	outlined chapter on pre-writing tasks	27	21177	22027	850
20-Feb	step 7, I wonder if enough anecdotes throughout, & clearly identified problems to solv	130	22027	24085	2058
21-Feb	finished up 7, outlined 8 so I have somewhere to go (not feeling 'it' today)	35	24085	24758	673
22-Feb	both rapid writing & pasting in (to be edited) previous writing, makes falsely huge worc	78	24758	27279	2521
23-Feb	with airplane time, I went back through to be sure I had enough examples to keep inte	186	27279	30840	3561
24-Feb	checked the bibliography and layout and emailed to my editor, fingers crossed!	42			0
		1735 minutes			30840

If I can just be brave enough to open that *.xls* file and write down the starting time, then I find that I can work hard on the project. And at the same time, I know I must write down the time I stop, and this commitment to record-keeping helps keep me on track. This same approach works with dieters: when they log everything they eat, they can more easily avoid eating sweets when they know they must write down the ingestion of an unhealthy cookie.

We all have rituals we follow, either consciously or unconsciously. For many of us, we follow a sequential morning ritual. We wake up, we brush our teeth, we get dressed, we make coffee, and we check our email. These things we likely never question or alter. *Busy Professors* also make use of rituals and habits to get good scholarly work done. Project-starting rituals, like opening a *.xls* time log or setting a Pomodoro technique timer, become a regular feature of being productive day after day.

Gotta-Do

Build 20-second barriers between you and things you want to avoid

Have courage to devote just 20 minutes to something in order to get started

Break up your day's important tasks with highly-constrained, short duration, brain-resetting tasks that are not email-related

Use frequently updated time logs to be accountable to yourself

STEP SEVEN:
Pre-write letters, committee tasks, and grading comments

Well-known *Busy Professors* are always being asked to do service tasks that do not build their CVs but are nonetheless important services to the broader profession. These time-consuming tasks include writing letters of recommendation, serving on committees, and externally evaluating promotion-seeking senior professors. The demands for these tasks only increase as *Busy Professors* become more notable and more senior as their career matures.

People depend on professors to produce evaluation materials. Imagine that top-tier student anxiously waiting for their busy advisor to get around to writing that required letter of recommendation they need to be considered for a job. Imagine that worried junior professor who needs one more article acceptance in order to apply for promotion from that busy reviewer. Imagine that administrator who needs that final committee report before they can enact a larger sabbatical policy for faculty from that busy committee chair. Why is it that overly busy professors apologize and say that they just can't find the time, whereas productive *Busy Professors* are magically able to make the time to get it done and done well?

We all have the same 24-hour day. Fortunately, *Busy Professors* have proven time-saving tactics they use to get more done in less time than their counterparts. Using these short-cut hacks allow *Busy Professors* to do what is required and get back to the intellectual endeavors they most want to do.

Pre-writing letters

Busy Professors generally take care of their own correspondence, as long gone are the days where a secretary would compose letters for us to sign from our fractured dictations. The key to keeping correspondence from taking over your life is to pre-write templates for letters you are going to have to write over and over again.

Consider an imaginary student who is applying for jobs and has asked you to provide an enthusiastically positive letter of recommendation. The key thing to remember here is that you will not be writing just one letter for the student, but perhaps tens of letters for the student. Moreover, each letter will have to be slightly different, as in one case you might be emphasizing the student's ability to teach, whereas in another you might be emphasizing the student's trajectory as an emerging scholar. Not to mention the strict due dates to which you must adhere, because if you miss them the student will not be considered for those jobs. Such a situation can present a real challenge for the ill-prepared busy professor, who is lucky to make most deadlines on the best of days. *Busy Professors* make this seemingly time-consuming task many times easier by pre-writing several letters, then rapidly deploying them, altering as needed.

The best letters of recommendation—those that result in a positive result for the requestor—are those that contain specific examples. Whereas hasty busy professors quickly write that the student has strong potential to be a good teacher, *Busy Professors* take time to give specific examples and paint a vivid picture of what experiencing that teacher's classroom looks like. In much the same way, when discussing a student's or colleague's research, provide a non-specialist description of the scholarly landscape and explain what about the emerging scholar's work is going to add to solving a critical question influencing the field.

Busy Professors are then quickly able to assemble and deploy a job-specific letter. If the target institution is a research-focused institution, then the paragraph describing specific examples of the research goes first, followed by specific examples related to teaching. If the target institution is a teaching-focused institution, then lead instead with the pre-written paragraph about teaching, and carefully consider whether to include any information about scholarship, because at some teaching-focused institutions, one's desire to engage in scholarship is considered a negative aspect.

Finally, always start a letter with a description of who you are and your qualifications to make a judgement. End your letter with seemingly personal commentary on the student's friendly demeanor and proven ability to work in a collaborative environment. All institutions want likeable people and carry the illusion that they themselves work in an institution that is highly supportive of collaborative work. In this way, *Busy Professors* can deploy strong and targeted letters of recommendation within minutes.

Being wise about committee appointments

The stated three pillars of academia are scholarship, teaching, and service. Although these three seem to be equivalent, I think we can all agree that they do not receive equal weight when performance reviews are conducted. If you are new to the profession, you might not realize that there are nearly unlimited opportunities, if not undue pressure, to conduct service activities and almost no reward. In fact, the most common criticism of busy professors is that "their high commitment to service activities is probably interfering with their ability to produce high-quality, creative scholarship." There is far too little credit given for service activities when it comes time for performance evaluations, and as a result, *Busy Professors* who want to have a rich intellectual life strictly limit how much service they do, particularly on their local campus. The reality is that there are far too many opportunities to serve and far too many liabilities for interfering with one's scholarship production. So, how do *Busy Professors* think about service?

When they must choose a committee assignment, *Busy Professors* focus on participating in scholarship and award committees. These committees exist at local and national levels within most professional societies. Such groups do not meet face-to-face frequently, if at all, and you get insight into what is really valued among academics within and outside your domain. Similarly, national advisory boards, such as those that guide research journals, also give *Busy Professors* national insight into the ever-evolving inner clockworks of academia and are not deeply time-consuming.

Unquestionably, some committees are more prolonged and intellectually draining than others. If forced to be on a traditional committee, *Busy Professors* quickly volunteer to sit on those that do not meet often. These are the *Committee on*

Committees or the *Nominations Committee*, which, like scholarship and award committees, rarely meet, and when they do, consider the wide range and domain of available faculty for appointments, allowing one to get to better know the broader community and still have important impacts. A *Busy Professor*'s favorite service committee is a professional society's best dissertation-of-the-year award committee because they get insight into what the latest and greatest scholarly minds are working on.

The most deceptively attractive committees that *Busy Professors* avoid, on the other hand, are the protracted committees engaging in conference or faculty retreat planning. Such committees provide only limited professional reward and rarely enhance one's CV. To be fair, such committees can be valuable, if kept in the right perspective. Probably the best committees to influence long-term success are those that increase a *Busy Professor*'s required social capital and help to expand their social network.

When considering joining a more time-consuming committee, it is critical that you are deeply interested in the work and results of the committee. If you are not fascinated by the committee's charge, then you will likely start to miss meetings, and the entire experience can become a negative one. Nonetheless, *Busy Professors* stringently avoid the strong temptation to volunteer to lead special sub-projects of any committee; instead, they attend regularly, are responsive, and learn the innerworkings and invisible poetical pitfalls that adorn the academy.

Unquestionably, the toughest decision a *Busy Professor* must make about service is whether to join a faculty hiring search committee. On the positive side, one quickly gets insight into how universities work, what departments value, the tacit agendas of fellow faculty members, and how to inadvertently get on someone's bad-side. It would be naïve to pretend that grudges and long-standing battle wounds do not exist among academics. On the negative side, these time-consuming hiring committees are also committed to helping entertain and recruit on-campus guests, which can completely overwhelm your schedule and scholarly productivity, even though you might get a few free meals out of the process. Unquestionably, hiring appropriately is the most important task a department, school, or college does, because good hiring makes for great colleagues and easy pathways through the tenure and promotion process, whereas poor hiring decisions are a long-standing drag on everyone. There is considerable truth in the mantra, "It is easier to hire than fire." Given all of this, *Busy Professors* are generally hesitant about joining a hiring committee and certainly avoid serving as chair.

If a *Busy Professor* is cajoled into a committee leadership role that requires gathering information or sub-reports from committee members and writing a final report, *Busy Professors* pre-write as much of the report as possible, including blanks for the final numbers and results.

Pre-writing requests and gentle reminders is a standard strategy for *Busy Professors* everywhere. When accepting a leadership task, take a few moments to figure out what pieces need to come together and in what sequence. Then, in a saved document, pre-write all the emails that need to go out and the reminders needed when busy professors fail to respond. Otherwise, you'll be aimlessly sitting at the computer saying, "Okay, who do I need to contact about this?" One can even pre-write much of the final report, leaving blank spaces for the information you are gathering.

Writing external evaluation reports

Because of their notoriety as an actively contributing member of the scholarly community, *Busy Professors* are often asked to conduct external evaluations of mid-career faculty or of programs. This is critical service to the academy, and it brings even more accolades from within and beyond the institution. Such tasks can bloom into unimaginably large tasks if you do not have a strict formula to follow every time you write an external evaluation. To be sure, *Busy Professors* always appropriately cut and paste the beginning and end of an external evaluation from previously written evaluations to save time.

Who are you? All external evaluation letters require the writer to establish credibility in the field. In addition to your time in rank and leadership positions held, *Busy Professors* also provide quantitative metrics, such as citation indices and number of publications, so that readers know to take your recommendation seriously.

What are the numerical quantitative markers of performance? Whether or not you believe in numbers and indices personally, university administrators and people outside your field take numbers seriously. To create an influential external evaluation, *Busy Professors* always provide as many objective-appearing numbers as possible. The reason for this is that once you have established the objective markers, you then and only then have permission to make a more qualitative, perhaps even widely subjective argument. If you do not provide the expected quantitative summary of markers, any impassioned qualitative assessment will likely be discarded. This requirement of numerical assessments—number of publications, number of pages, number of citations, number of conference presentations, number of national committees, number of courses taught, values of teaching evaluation scores—is even more important when low numbers reflect a weak argument. These numbers and index-values are easy to acquire online through *GoogleScholar* or *ResearchGate* and providing them for the reader indicates you are being comprehensive in your review. In contrast, minimizing such issues indicates a red flag and negates one's following qualitative arguments.

What is your objective-sounding, qualitative assessment? Only after the numbers have been established will a qualitative assessment be taken seriously. When I was much younger, I collected baseball cards. On the back of every baseball card are two sections. The first section denotes the player's numerical statistics: games played, batting average, homeruns, stolen bases, strikeouts, wins, and losses. The second section is a narrative paragraph explaining the statistics. For example, the player might have many wins because he was on the World Series winning baseball team. Alternatively, low scores might be the result of an early season-ending injury. The qualitative paragraph explains or explains away the players' performance numbers. Whether in professional sports or in academia, a helpful external assessment provides an interpretation of the numbers to a non-specialist reader.

In this qualitative section, *Busy Professors* provide context for the numbers. Highly productive professors in some sub-fields of physics produce a single paper every other year with a single authorship, whereas in other sub-fields of physics, 10 co-authored papers per year is the bare minimum required to call yourself a physicist. In other fields a journal simply called "letters" is the discipline standard of rigor despite its seemingly informal moniker, whereas other disciplines expect productive academics to produce books from notable publishers. As an external reviewer with credibility, you are the person that explains the evidence to an out-of-field specialist whether or not the person or program is actually influencing the field and attaining national prominence. This is particularly important in cases where a scholar is highly active at professional conferences but not rapidly moving their work into archival journals. Additionally, this is where the external evaluator makes a case for where the scholar is publishing; as in many fields, including mine, the most influential journal everyone reads isn't formally a certifiable tier-1 journal.

What is the clear, summative evaluation statement? At the end of every external evaluation, the reader is expecting a clear judgement statement. Such statements can be qualified as, "When comparing the available evidence to your institution's guidelines, my judgement is _____." If you want to be taken seriously, your evaluative judgement cannot in any way be qualified by comparing the institution to another. In other words, *Busy Professors* who want their review to be taken seriously would never write, "would merit promotion at my institution," as such an inappropriate comparison negates an entire review wholesale. The individual or program is at a certain institution with specific guidelines that only apply to that institution.

Grading student work

In my own academic life, pre-writing possible feedback to students has been the biggest time-saver I've ever used. Before *Busy Professors* ever grade a single paper, imagine what to say to the student who has written the perfect solution and write them a note that could potentially be copy and pasted into a feedback textbox for all top-performing students in a paperless class.

For example:

Our goal this week was to fully understand the life cycle of Sun-like stars. Many students imagine that our Sun will turn into a black hole, but your answers clearly indicate that you have the right idea that when our Sun depletes its usable fuel supply, it will become a planetary nebula. I thought your depiction of _____ was particularly well constructed. Overall, your answers are clear and mostly accurate—you should probably double check your answers against the posted solutions—and you receive full points on this assignment. You did a great job on this assignment and are meeting my expectations. Keep up this level of quality and you'll do great on the next exam.

Kindly notice that there is a <u>blank</u> where *Busy Professors* can easily and individually personalize feedback for the student.

The next step is to skim through a few papers to see what the most common errors are. A *Busy Professor* is then in a position to create a second pre-written response, which can be rapidly deployed by copy and pasting into those students' feedback textboxes. For example:

Our goal this week was to fully understand the life cycle of Sun-like stars. Your submitted answers suggest that you do not yet fully understand the sequence of end-states when stars run out of useable fuel and your answers include some critical mistakes. For example, _____. Please carefully compare your responses to the posted solutions and if you do not fully understand how to correct your errors, please come see me in my office for a few minutes, and we'll get you straightened out before the next exam. You earned partial points for this submission.

Again, you should notice that there is another <u>blank</u> where *Busy Professors* can quickly insert personalized feedback for the student. For most purposes, usually two or three pre-written feedback paragraphs are all I need to rapidly provide written feedback to all my students.

Part of my motivation in what I've written here for feedback is due to my observation that my poorly performing students rarely read the feedback sufficiently and carefully enough to learn from it. As a result, I ask students to review the posted answer solutions, and then if they do not fully understand the mistakes they made and how to correct them, then to please come see me in my office. My thinking here is that I can better explain to students face-to-face in just five minutes what I have previously been unsuccessful in doing when giving them a long-written description that requires a considerable amount of my time to construct. Sometimes, my feedback is quite vague, but urgent. For example:

There are some real problems with your homework assignment. Please schedule a time to come by my office because it will be easier to help you face-to-face.

As mentioned earlier, *Busy Professor*s also use this pre-writing strategy for completing the day's email processing to make responses look less frantic and more thoughtful.

Hey _____: Thanks for sending me an email about this. I'm sorry I am a bit slow in responding, but I'm working hard to not check my email as often. Next time, if you need a faster response, call my cell at 520-975-1374 (I don't text well).

<insert response>

You don't need to email me back on this unless something here doesn't make sense. NRN (No Reply Necessary), Tim

Use these time-saving strategies to get more done in less time so you can focus on the things that you really love doing and being with the people you really want to be with.

Gotta-Do

Pre-write letters, then liberally cut and paste for future ones

Cautiously consider accepting any committee appointments

Consistently use a formula of quantitative evidence before qualitative evidence for evaluation reports

Pre-write possible student feedback responses

STEP EIGHT:
Every talk or poster becomes a paper

Far too many busy professors fail to publish papers or complete whichever tasks are required for them to move forward professionally even when they want to because they do not fully understand the sequence of events required to make large-scale projects like published papers happen. *Busy Professors* recognize that writing a paper is mechanical, and planning and perseverance are the more difficult parts. Just like you will never get in good physical shape if you wait until you feel inspired to go to the gym, which never happens, *Busy Professors* work on their projects whether or not they feel like it. If you know what you are up against, you are much more likely to be successful in overcoming the inherent barriers in scholarly publishing.

Generating new ideas

Some busy professors have too many ideas for what to create and write about, whereas others do not have even one. Prolific *Busy Professors* realize that ideas for publishing stem entirely from clearly identifying problems and missing links in the scholarly landscape, and they immerse themselves in *questions*.

Where do *Busy Professors* find questions that need answers? Depending on your field, the most common place is probably from the scholarly literature of journal articles and critical literature reviews written by others. Scholarly authors are supposed to be summarizing what is known about an idea and what is still unknown or unexplored about an idea before they present their own ideas or data. It is here in the opening pages of an article where *Busy Professors* find unanswered questions begging to be addressed. Alternatively, articles in many fields provide a final, short section on future research directions needed that are worth considering.

The fastest place to find intellectual questions that need answers is at professional conferences, usually in the featured conference keynote talk. Keynote speakers by and large are leaders in the field who are more willing than most junior scholars to talk about what they still haven't gotten around to figuring out yet. *Busy Professors* may screw up the courage at conferences the seek out and talk to these leaders about nagging, unanswered questions, which is in stark contrast to busy professors, who often want to grab a keynote speaker's attention, so they can momentarily validate themselves by sharing what they know rather than learning from an expert. Think about how many post-talk question and answer sessions have busy professors intellectually showboating and making statements, rather than taking the unique opportunity to ask a question and listen. In short, I see far too many busy professors going to conferences simply to talk and far too few going to learn. *Busy Professors* go to conferences primarily to learn and to share their ideas for rapid feedback.

Make a presentation at every conference

Each year, you should plan on attending at least one national conference where you will make at least one scholarly presentation. Uninformed busy professors think that participating in a conference means going and quietly listening to speakers from the back of the room, and that they deserve travel funds from their institution to support this trip. They vaguely justify their trip by saying, "I want to keep up on trends in my field."

Busy Professors believe that going to a conference means immersing oneself in questions of the discipline and learning from other scholars. They go with the specific intention of interacting and learning from scholars who capture their attention or whom they have heard speak in the past. And *Busy Professors* always present a paper when attending a conference with the goal of getting people to punch bullet holes in their thinking, their research plans, or their ideas. Busy professors speaking at conferences hope that no one really questions their work, which is the absolute worst thing that can happen to a *Busy Professor*, who seeks questions that provide new insights. No questions at the end of a talk does not mean that the work is intellectually clever and perfectly well done: no questions at the end of a *Busy*

Professor's talk implies that there is insufficient scholarly substance in the work worth debating or improving.

Don't know what to present? Present a paper on a critical literature review where you summarize what is known about an idea, summarize what is not yet known, and highlight the holes between the two and propose ideas for how one might explore the space between what is known and what is unknown. Being prompted for an explanation why this specific area is important for the field to explore in the first place makes for an engaging talk at any conference.

Convert every talk into a publication

In days gone by, when scholars were not tethered to their smart phones, annual conferences were critical to advancing the field. The rate of publication was at best a few papers per year, usually much less, and the speed of publication to print was incredibly slow, often taking more than a year. Moreover, doing literature reviews were incredibly difficult, as one often had to wait weeks on Interlibrary Loan to mail an article to read colleagues' work. Professional conferences provided an avenue for people to more quickly move work forward, and conference talks would add a little more to an idea each year, resulting in some single publication years down the road, representing a single article, representing years of one's accumulated conference presentations. Those scholars have long since retired.

In today's academia, most scholars have goals of publishing at least one paper each year with dreams of many more. Publishing a paper is physically easier, fiscally cheaper, and less time-consuming than ever before. Most of us never go to the library; instead, we conduct our literature reviews from our Internet-connected computer or smart phone. We can skim tens of articles in the time it took our predecessors to load up a microfiche in the library to eventually find a single article. I'm not saying today is better or worse, but what I am saying is that the speed has increased. The result is that today's scholars often try to publish articles in *lowest publishable units*, or LPUs. Personally, I'm not advocating or denigrating publishing one's work in LPUs, but it is a common trend.

In any event, *Busy Professors* use each conference presentation as a completed and detailed outline of a soon-to-be published journal article. It takes a tremendous amount of intellectual effort to put together a talk, and *Busy Professors* never waste this energy investment. Some *Busy Professors* even use their smart phone to audio record their presentations and pay someone across the ocean to quickly transcribe their spoken presentation into a text document. Although humans do not speak using the same words and sentence structures that are used in formal writing, having a document with all the ideas in place often serves as a huge head start on getting a manuscript out the door, particularly for those scholars who do not enjoy the writing process.

Convert every formal journal article into an informal publication

When you consider the considerable effort that goes into getting a formal, refereed journal article in press, it should be worth more than a single line on your CV. In fact, an article should be worth more than just two lines on your CV—one for the preceding pre-publication conference presentation and one for the published article itself. Smart *Busy Professors* who want to get as much bang for their buck always take a little time to write a very short version of their published paper's research and results for non-specialists for the university's alumni fundraising magazine, for their college's newsletter, or even for the local newspaper. These tasks do not take very long, and the impact on one's notoriety can tremendously be worth the small investment. *Busy Professors* know that letting people know about their work isn't bragging but is instead incredibly helpful in the institution, receiving continued support for being relevant and active community contributors. More to the point, taxpayers and college donors want to know that they are supporting a winning institution, and advertising your successful efforts goes a long way in helping to improve perceptions. The same goes for when you've won a grant award competition.

If you've ever overseen a professional society's newsletter, receiving a crisply written, unsolicited contribution for the newsletter or webpage is like mana from heaven. This is particularly true for smaller regional organizations you might be a member of who desperately need good news to share, and *Busy Professors* take a few moments to share their good fortunes.

Don't waste your summer break

Few professors love writing every day, but producing creative scholarship is one of the markers of success. Successful *Busy Professors* don't worry about if they should be writing because they know they are scheduled to write from 8-10 am, for example, and don't feel guilty about not writing at 11am, or 3 pm, or 9 pm, or on weekends. Hopeful busy professors tell their colleagues that they are looking forward to winter break, spring break, or summer break so that they can finally get some writing done. These well-meaning busy professors hold on to a hope that they can binge write in just a few weeks an entire year's worth of writing goals. Ever talk to those busy professors after break? Their honest binge-writing intentions are never realized. Don't fall into this trap.

At the end of the school term before summer break, busy professors feel tired and disconnected from their families. Most busy professors "know" that they need to mentally and physically rest in order to feel motivated for the fall term, so they either take time off and try not think about their job at all, or at the other extreme, frantically try to read everything and write everything they need to in a short three-month period to catch up. Unfortunately, both approaches are woefully ineffective.

What do *Busy Professors* choose to do each summer that is different from their busy professor counterparts? Scholarly research on productivity is clear that the way *Busy Professors* keep having insightfully creative ideas is to write—and to write a lot. Busy professors who want to be clearheaded with lots of ideas need to spend at least an hour every day of the summer writing. Just 750 words five days a week will do magic, but most busy professors won't choose to do it because they either believe it's too many words or not enough words to be meaningful. As it turns out, 750 words really isn't very much, but it really adds up when done over a 100-day summer.

Busy Professors who write prolifically take well-deserved breaks during winter break, spring break, or parts of summer break, and spend that time in healthy recovery doing hobbies or enjoying time with friends. This way, they can stay mentally sharp and productive during the rest of the year. *Busy Professors* do this by writing a little every day, rather than attempting a binge-writing approach that never works.

How do *Busy Professors* stay disciplined and on-track when the kids are out of school and the weather is invitingly warm? Ben Franklin was right about getting up in the morning: "Early to rise makes one healthy, wealthy, and wise." The most productive *Busy Professors* get up early—even when on a beachside vacation. Hal Elrod's book *The Miracle Morning* gives clear instructions about how to spend one hour a day when everyone else is asleep to become the most productive person you can be. After getting up early and writing, a *Busy Professor* then has from 7 am onward to do whatever they want to do unrelated to their scholarly job.

In the end, the most important strategy any productive *Busy Professor* can have is a habitual routine for all times of the year. The most productive *Busy Professors* know ahead of time what they're doing at 8:30 am every day and what they will be doing at 11 am, and they work hard not to confuse the two. Consistently, *Busy Professors* carefully script their morning schedules before the inevitable chaos of the day sweeps away the best of intentions.

Gotta-Do

Get new ideas from literature and conference presentations

Attend conferences for learning and receiving critical feedback

Make conference presentations every year

Convert every conference presentation into a publication

Covert every publication or winning grant proposal into a newsletter or magazine contribution

Write early mornings in the summer so that the rest of the day is yours to spend recovering and nurturing relationships

---

STEP NINE:
Use Smart Phone Apps to Build Your CV

The most effective *Busy Professors* among us spend the first five minutes of each day planning out their day so they can focus on what is most important. They know what time they will start working, what they will be working on at 10 am and 2 pm, and perhaps most importantly, they know precisely what time they will be going home. Sure, interruptions will happen, but an effective plan takes this into account: if you have meeting after meeting scheduled every second of the day, you shouldn't include finding time to write a paper on your daily plan because that isn't going to happen. Moreover, before *Busy Professors* go out the door at the end of the day, they take five minutes to note what they will do first thing tomorrow morning; that way, they don't have to worry about work all evening, which might otherwise interrupt valuable rest and family time. Just like successfully cleaning your house requires that you adopt a mantra of everything has its place and everything goes in its place, *Busy Professors* utilize the notion that all tasks have a scheduled time in which to be dealt with and scheduled time is when those tasks get done. It is easier said than done, but when done, feels easy.

This discussion might feel like I'm suggesting that new opportunities don't unexpectedly come up, that challenges do not appear to interrupt one's flow, or that great ideas don't suddenly present themselves in the middle of working on something else. It is absurd to think that a *Busy Professor* might not have a great idea about Project A when they are supposed to be working on Project B. This most certainly does happen. *Busy Professors* have ready-to-go procedures in place to deal with these interruptions, and most of us make use of our smart phones to gently pick up and move these interruptions out of the way to a more useful place. The goal here is to have systems to capture and store for easy retrieval of brilliant ideas that come up but can be dealt with later.

Before talking about smart phone apps that *Busy Professors* use to capture tangentially related ideas and resources that appear when working, I would be remiss if I didn't mention the benefit of keeping a small, pocket-sized notebook to jot down ideas, so they aren't lost. In fact, all *Busy Professors* I know keep their notebook by their bedside, so if they suddenly wake in the middle of the night with an idea, they can record it in their notebooks and feel safe going back to sleep, having captured the idea. The advantage of the paper-and-pencil notebook is that it does not require a charged battery, nor does it emit brain-stimulating blue light as a smart phone does, which makes it harder for one to go back to sleep easily.

Smart phone apps for *Busy Professors*

Recognizing that new and improved smart phone apps show up all the time, there are timeless categories of smart phone apps that *Busy Professors* need to capture ideas and resources that appear. Personally, I like simple and free apps that mirror themselves across my various devices: smart phone, tablet, laptop, and desktop. I keep *NotePad* or *WordPad* simple text apps easily available for anything I need to write down quickly before I forget it. And it goes without saying that *Busy Professors* need to be able to access their calendar across devices.

TO DO list. There are countless TO DO list apps out there, some with endless bells and whistles. Personally, I use *Wunderlist* because I can quickly add TO DO items with optional due dates and sub-folders. I use subfolders so that I can separate out short 5-minute TO DO tasks that I can quickly complete when I've got a few spare minutes and people to *telephone* tasks for when I'm waiting in an airport or traveling in a car or train.

Saved napkin notes. At the end of most professional conferences, I have a stack of folded bar napkins with notes, graphs, and lists that I need to do something with when I get home. I am always ending up with tons of little pieces of paper with written notes or pointers to websites I really need to come back to. I inevitably get suggestions for movies I need to see or books I need to read. *Busy Professors* need to have a virtual filing cabinet to capture all these things for later retrieval. Personally, I use *Evernote* because I can upload or email myself almost anything, including cell phone pictures of those pesky napkins, scans of passports, business cards, directions to friends' houses, PDF articles, and website resources that will someday inform my writing or teaching.

Most important is the virtual filing cabinet where *Busy Professors* put everything they will need for completing their annual performance review. When I first started out as an academic, it was recommended to me that I keep a drawer in my desk where I toss in everything I'll need as evidence to document my tenure application—published articles, letters of appreciation for service, and student evaluations. A virtual filing cabinet is the modern equivalent of that desk drawer.

Timer and alarm clock. *Busy Professors* struggle just like everyone else to sit down and start on a project. Using an app's stopwatch, timer, and alarm clock is highly valuable when you vow to work on something for, say, 20 minutes. A smart phone app is a great way to keep track of time during that 20-minute commitment. An alarm clock is also essential for waking *Busy Professors* so that they can get started slaying the day's dragons before everyone else gets up and starts making requests for their time and attention. Moreover, it reminds *Busy Professors*, after they get into the flow of writing, when it is time to stop writing. Once you start adhering to a project schedule, magic really does happen. I particularly like an app called *30/30* that allows you to sequence a bunch of timers to work one after the other.

Motivation apps. Even the most disciplined of *Busy Professors* need to see progress to stay motivated. Smart phone apps that list your daily goals and keep track of how often you meet them are particularly helpful. At the moment, I like *Coach.me* for keeping track of daily goals, like practicing my ukulele. Similarly, I use *Quit That!* to help me keep track of things I do not want to do anymore, like not checking my email before I've written 750 words. And for meditation and relaxation practice, I find *Insight Timer*, *Take a Break*, and *HeadSpace* to be consistently useful when I need to reset my attitude.

Nudgemail. Although *Busy Professors* intuitively know that one's email inbox is a terrible place to keep TO DO items, sometimes TO DO items end up there. All of us are always tempted to do the task that is right in front of us rather than the

TO DO task that is most important. *Busy Professors* leverage this by being sure the right things jump up in our field of view at the right time. One strategy is to email yourself a TO DO item at a specific time and have it show up on the correct day, like a reminder for a colleague's birthday. I make frequent use of nudgemail.com. If I need to remember to stop by the store for milk, I email myself a reminder that says "get milk" to 430pm@nudgemail.com or Wednesday@nudgemail.com and magically it shows up in my inbox at the prescribed time. I use this reminder system nearly every day in one way or another.

Improving performance at one's desk

By getting their life organized and putting everything in its place using smart phone apps, *Busy Professors* are left with the prospect of actually getting things done when they are supposed to be done, if not early. So, given the mobility of smart phones and laptops, just where do *Busy Professors* get their work done? It might surprise you to learn that *Busy Professors* often get work done in their office at their desk.

Have you ever heard people say that they have their best ideas when in the shower or driving in the car? Perhaps you yourself have said, "I think best when I'm walking around the building, far from my desk." This notion should strike you as incredibly odd because you are not actually being paid to shower, or drive, or walk. In fact, you are being paid to be a productively creative scholar at work. Of all the places in the world to be creative and productive, it should most often be at your desk.

The single best location where *Busy Professors* have everything they need to be productive is their clean desk in their neatly organized office. Your desk is supposedly where you have best access to your calendar, your computer, your files, your books, sticky notes, index cards, pens, cell phone charger, highlighters, and a stapler. Most offices have a telephone and immediate access to one's peers and support staff, who are inarguably an often critically important resource. Some people go as far as adding attractive plants, family pictures, an inviting bowl of candy, comfortable chairs, their favorite music, nuanced lighting, and inspirational awards on the wall. Yet, with all these accoutrements, why do so many people "think" better elsewhere?

The Busy Professor

Time is an incredibly important and limited resource, and *Busy Professors* are masters at successfully managing their time. At its core, effective time management is about two things: doing the most important job first and eliminating distractions that keep you from getting that most important job done—like writing articles, creating engaging learning tasks for class, or creating new policies that improve budgets for everyone. Unfortunately, busy professors often unwittingly set up their offices to welcome unwanted distractions that keep them from completing their number one prioritized task.

The first step *Busy Professors* use when redesigning a productive office space is to clearly identify what specifically distracts them from getting their most important tasks done, and it is well worth committing to a week of making notes of those distractions. Because barriers to effective productivity sneak up on us over time, it often takes an active and purposeful effort to figure out what distracts us. The table below describes some common distractions and a possible time management hack to improve the situation.

Unwanted Distraction	*Busy Professor* Strategy
Email	Allocate two blocks of time to respond to email, & turn it off otherwise
Text Messages	Put your phone charger out of reach of your desk on other side of room & silence it
Papers to Grade	Put distracting papers & mail in a box with a lid out of sight to grade when scheduled
Chatty Colleagues	Place stacks of paper on your chairs & remove any candy bowls; hold headphones in your hands ready to reinsert when they take a breath
Social Media	Put 30 min. on your calendar each day to engage in social media & get a timer

"Just need a second"	Place sign on closed door that says, "Writing with headphones on, please knock loudly" for 2 hours each day
Noisy hallway	Ask for noise-reduction headphones for birthday (you are hard to buy for anyway)
Too messy to find anything	Clean your desk on Friday afternoon calendar when you are largely unproductive

Busy Professors take the time to get good at time management and use smart phone tools, so they can spend more time doing what they love most about the job. No professor gets promoted by filing committee reports, attending meetings, grading papers, or balancing research budgets. Sure, these things are important, but not as important as doing what you love about your job: writing more, reading more, spending more time in a research setting, more creative teaching, and working more closely with students and colleagues.

Gotta-Do

Keep a paper-and-pencil notebook next to your bed to safely release brilliant ideas that are keeping you awake at night

Use smart phone apps to mirror information across your smart phone, tablet, laptop, and desktop

Put barriers in place to make your office desk your happily productive space

Place a sign on your door that says, "Writing with headphones, please knock loudly" if you want to be left alone

---

STEP TEN:
Get a non-work life if you want to be more productive at work

Do the most successful *Busy Professors* work 40 hours each week? Do they work 60 hours each week? Do they work all the time, giving up sleep? Nope, *Busy Professors* make certain they do not work more than 40 hours each week because they know that creative brains need rest and recovery time to stay sharp.

Consider this seemingly unrelated example: if you have a chain saw for cutting down trees, you cannot use that chain saw continuously and expect it to keep working. In fact, a poorly working chain saw is even harder to use than a traditional hand saw. To work properly, even the most expensive chain saws need regular downtime for cooling and require engine cleaning and careful sharpening of the cutting surfaces. Like an expensive chain saw, the brain of a *Busy Professor* also needs to regularly think about things other than work to be more productive than their overworked and unproductive busy professor colleagues, who regularly spend 50 or 60 or more hours per week immersed in their unending work-related TO DO lists.

So, how do *Busy Professors* get everything done that needs to be done in just 40 hours per week? As is consistently repeated here, devoting oneself to structure creates freedom. The only way to do this is to schedule when things are to be done and do those things only when they are scheduled.

Strictly limit time allocated to class preparation

Most *Busy Professors* love teaching. Teaching is an opportunity to revisit and think deeply about the big ideas of a discipline in ways that help novice learners understand complex ideas. No one has ever disputed the notion that the best way to learn deeply about a concept is to teach it to someone else. *Busy Professors* are generally ravenous learners, often making them engaging teachers. As a result, one can easily spend all their available time devoted to teaching tasks, like class preparation. Teaching is one of those things wherein there is never sufficient time to do.

To combat this very real issue, *Busy Professors* must strictly limit the amount of time each week they allocate to class preparation. We all wish we had more time to find that perfect illustration or to better fine-tune an exam, no matter how much time is available.

One of the immutable principles of life is that any given task will expand and take up all the time allotted to it. The way this plays out for professors is that if you give yourself two hours to prepare a lecture, the task will take two hours. If instead you give yourself four hours to prepare a lecture, the task will then take four hours. In other words, things in life tend to take up the precise amount of time one allocates to it. As a result, no matter how much *Busy Professors* love teaching, they adhere to strict time limits for how much time they will spend preparing for class, recognizing it isn't enough but will have to suffice. Otherwise, class preparation will expand to take up all the available time, which isn't okay if teaching is only a portion of your responsibilities.

Read newspaper headlines but not articles

Academics are often notably poor conversationalists. This leads for awkward moments of silence when sitting in a meeting room waiting for the consistently late busy professor, who agreed to serve as chair for yet another committee. How do *Busy Professors* fill the uncomfortable void when there isn't anything to talk about? *Busy Professors* always take 30 seconds of each day when traveling to the office to quickly note that day's newspaper or web newsfeed headlines. However, what is different here is that *Busy Professors* never actually read the articles following the headlines. In this way, *Busy Professors* can break awkward silences by revealing that they noticed a headline earlier in the day but haven't yet had time to read the accompanying article and are curious if anyone else in the room knows what the story is all about. This strategy almost always gets a conversation going and grants you the appearance of a great conversationalist while letting other folks feel good about themselves by telling you what they know.

Get a hobby

Academics are extremely high risk for being terribly boring individuals. They either talk incessantly about the things they are interested in or don't know what to say. You've probably heard it said that experts know more and more about less and less until they know everything there is to know about nothing. Does that sound like someone you would like to hang out with socially?

If you don't have an enthusiastic answer when someone asks you what your hobbies are, you are in trouble. *Busy Professors* never say that they do not have enough time to have hobbies, unless they are parents of quintuplets or some other such blessing. You need to make time for a hobby of some kind—cool your overworked brain by focusing on something else occasionally, which incidentally will encourage you to become a more interesting individual. Don't know where to start? Try an Internet search for something akin to "I need a new hobby."

Host a monthly spaghetti dinner party

Just like you need to purposefully make time for your specific academic tasks, you also need to purposefully make time to nurture relationships with other human beings. When you were in elementary school, friendships just seemed to naturally happen; as an adult, friendships are more difficult to come by. Adult friendships need to be intentionally sought after and frequently nurtured, particularly in the academic world where people move across country frequently.

The easiest way to start a circle of friends is to be on the alert for four people from four different departments across campus and invite them to your house for a casual spaghetti dinner. A box of spaghetti and a can of pasta sauce only costs a few dollars, and when served comes with few expectations. You can even open a cheap jug of red wine if you are so inclined.

You do not need to hide your agenda here of finding a circle of friends. Everyone could use more friends. And after a three-hour dinner with your new friends, propose doing it again next month and ask each of them to bring a friend, expanding the size of the group. After a few months, some folks will consistently come, others will drop out, and new friends will appear. I promise you that you'll be surprised how large and fun these informal dinner parties become, as long as you keep things on the cheap to lower social pressure. Eventually, these friends will show up on the university tenure and promotion committee or on award-selection committees, and you need to be known outside your own department. In work communities where everyone has a high IQ, the thing that separates one professor from another is their ability to nurture social networks, and *Busy Professors* place a high value on having an active social network.

Many time management books out there talk about strategies to attain a work-life balance. This is clearly something that we all desire, or else there wouldn't be so many books on the market proposing solutions. In the end, achieving work-life balance is important for *Busy Professors* for at least two reasons. One, academics need ways to rest and restore their brains, so they can recover and have brilliant ideas again tomorrow. The second reason is that academics need to think about things other than work. Happiness depends on having meaningful relationships with other human beings, and you can't even start down the road of having lasting relationships if you have nothing more to talk about than your work.

Gotta-Do

Strictly limit the time allocated for class preparation each week

Become a better conversationalist by quickly glancing at news headlines each morning

Get a hobby so you have something to talk about besides work, and rest your brain

Have the courage to host extended dinner parties to build a social network

---

NEXT STEPS:
Beyond the Ten Steps

One might summarize the *Busy Professor's* TEN STEPS as nothing more than "a draconian approach to eliminating distractions." Although I would prefer it be characterized in more nuanced and positive perspective, I must admit that, unquestionably, in order to have the freedom to do what you find most important, you *must* adopt structures that serve as barriers to the relentless daily whirlwind that keeps your dreams of productivity and happiness from being a reality.

One of the privileges of being a professor is the opportunity to travel to exotic and non-exotic locations around the world, often on someone else's credit card. Traveling to present at conferences to advance your scholarship or serving on national review boards is unquestionably an important component to gaining a national and international reputation. Yet, when I ask my most senior of mentors what one thing they would have done differently if they had to do it all over again would be, they consistently say, "Travel less." I think what they mean is this: on one level, these senior sages are saying that traveling too much is exhausting and interferes with one's ability to be a productive *Busy Professor* because it is difficult to keep your productivity schedule intact.

More importantly, I think on another level what largely underlies their notion is that too much travel takes away from cultivating meaningful and ongoing close relationships that human beings need to achieve happiness. Unfortunately, divorce rates are quite high among academics, mostly because of poorly nurtured relationships. Far too many busy professors are too busy to spend meaningful time with their kids. Or when overworked busy professor parents are physically present, their thoughts often place them somewhere else, which is essentially the same as being absent. It is easy to forget that we don't own our children; rather, we are borrowing them for an incredibly short time before they grow up and leave our nest.

One doesn't have to physically travel to be mentally absent from their friends and family. The primary difference between an unscheduled busy professor and a productive *Busy Professor* is that *Busy Professors* are never so busy and so overcommitted that they cannot be thoughtful and considerate of other human beings. Steve Maraboli is always cautious of people who respond to a universal "how are you?" with "busy" because "when someone tells you they are too 'busy'… It's not a reflection of their schedule; it's a reflection of YOUR spot on their schedule."

Can you recall how you feel when you call a business' customer service desk and are put on hold with a recording that says, "Your call is very important to us. Your call will be answered in the order it was received. Your anticipated wait time is 29 minutes." Does that make you feel like your call is very important to them? I didn't think so.

If your favorite thing about being an academic is creative scholarship and mentoring students, then that is what you should be spending your time on, and it should show up on your calendar that way. Similarly, if family is important to you, family time should be clearly reflected on your schedule. No matter what you passionately say and believe about how important someone is to you, the priority you place on someone is easily observable by noticing how you allocate your time.

For me, as I work toward becoming the best *Busy Professor* I can be, I am moved by the unattributed quote, "My greatest fear is that I'll look back on my life and not know what I've done with it." The limited number of years we have to be creative contributors to our scholarly community is far too short and goes by far too fast. If you want to be able to look back on your academic life, you need to work on a legacy a little bit every single day, whether you feel inspired and motivated to do it or not. Some days you will not feel like it, but in the same way you cannot fix your health by binge-exercising only during school breaks, academics cannot have the intellectual life they dream of by *only* dreaming about it. It's your life to do with as you wish, so make your plan and make it happen by prioritizing it.

BIBLIOGRAPHY:
For Further Reading

Ready for advanced time management skills? Try

> Merrill, A. R., & Merrill, R. (2004). *Life matters: Creating a dynamic balance of work, family, time, & money.* McGraw Hill Professional.

> Covey, S. R., Merrill, A. R., & Merrill, R. R. (1995). *First things first.* Simon and Schuster.

> Allen, D. (2015). *Getting things done: The art of stress-free productivity.* Penguin.

Ready to understand the cognitive science behind building new habits of practice? Try

> Duhigg, C. (2013). *The Power of Habit: Why we do what we do and how to change.* Random House.

> Silvia, P. J. (2007). *How to write a lot: A practical guide to productive academic writing.* American Psychological Association.

Ready to become financially secure? Try

> Bach, D. (2005). *The automatic millionaire: A powerful one-step plan to live and finish rich.* Crown Pub.

> Stanley, T. J., & Danko, W. D. (2010). *The millionaire next door: The surprising secrets of America's wealthy.* Taylor Trade Publishing.

Ready to become physically fit and mentally healthy? Try

Crowley, C., & Lodge, H. S. (2007). *Younger Next Year: Live Strong, Fit, and Sexy—Until You're 80 and Beyond.* Workman Publishing.

Medina, J. (2014). *Brain rules: 12 principles for surviving and thriving at work, home, and school.* Pear Press.

ABOUT THE AUTHOR

Dr. Tim Slater is an internationally respected scholar in science education. Formally trained as an astronomer, he is the Editor-in-Chief of the *Journal of Astronomy & Earth Sciences Education*, has co-authored 16 books, has been awarded nearly $20 million dollars in grants, and has more than 100 peer-reviewed scientific articles. He is the University of Wyoming Excellence in Higher Education Endowed Chair of Science Education and a Senior Scientist at the international CAPER Center for Astronomy & Physics Education Research. Known widely as the "Professor's Professor," Dr. Slater has provided workshops on innovative teaching and successful career management to thousands of college professors worldwide. In order to figure out how to do all of this, he has developed exceptional skills in time management, and he shares many of his lessons learned about increasing scholarly productivity in his latest book, *The Busy Professor*.

If you'd like to schedule The Busy Professor to come speak to your group, please contact us on the web at TheBusyProfessor.com or via email at TheBusyProfessor@CAPERteam.com

NOTES